THE INDEPENDENT LEARNER'S GUIDE TO
SUCCESSFUL HOME-SCHOOLING

FAYE PAIGE

ONYX PUBLISHING

First published in 2020 by Onyx Publishing, an imprint of
Notebook Publishing of Notebook Group Limited, 20–22 Wenlock
Road, London, N1 7GU.

www.notebookpublishing.co

ISBN: 9781913206406

A CIP catalogue record for this book is available
from the British Library.

Typeset by Onyx Publishing.

CONTENTS

AUTHOR'S NOTE

I HAD ALWAYS LOVED school.

Over the course of my primary school years, my self-esteem was high and I would walk straight-backed into a room of adults, confident of my own capabilities, maturity, and intellect. I had a natural curiosity in academics and loved to learn, this automatically putting me in the good books of my teachers. As an avid reader, I was advanced with my English, my struggles in Maths thus more than compensated for in my teachers' wants to see me succeed, and, as much as I was by no means popular, I was generally (I would like to think!) well-liked by the majority of my peers, and carried a small circle of friends with me throughout my childhood.

As (ironically!) a great many of us often were in our younger years, I was dubbed a 'gifted' child—by family and teachers alike—, and it felt like my primary objective throughout my younger years was to fulfil this title. As I am sure any of my family members and long-term friends would tell you, I was quite a serious child from the get-go: I favoured learning over play; one-to-one discussion over group chatter; books over TV and video games. I was introverted and anxiety-ridden outside of the classroom—especially around those my own age—, but was reassured and confident in the world of academia and adult conversation.

In summary, school had always been a safe haven for me: it was in my comfort zone, and was a place I knew my potential was recognised, my voice was heard, and everything had an order—and because of this, I looked forward to secondary school as a sort of extended, perfected version of my beloved primary school: specialised teachers, more peers to befriend, more challenging lesson content, and more independence within my daily routine.

By the time the much-anticipated first day of Year 7 had rolled around, I'd accumulated the perfect image of what I *knew* my next five years were going to entail: I imagined myself flourishing academically whilst still getting the 'typical teenage experience' we all anticipate in our younger years, filled with glamour, a significant other, parties, a ream of friends, lazy summer afternoons, and cosy winter nights in. I would find a group of like-minded people within the first couple of weeks and enjoy my classes filled with academic, mature students, and would be well-known and well-respected across my year. I had always craved social approval, and it was this that spurred my hopes and expectations of my adolescent years.

Of course, things didn't exactly pan out like this: within just a few weeks of my time in Year 7, I slowly but surely began to encounter a wealth of problems I had not foreseen during my countdown to September: some of which being the growing pains that commonly occur during that awkward period of change and self-discovery accompanying the onset of adolescence; others more personal and complex.

The former generally took the form of my social circle: whilst I did certainly develop some close friendships during my time in secondary school, I found myself not only confused but irritated by the social dynamics I was surrounded with. Suddenly, the majority of the relationships unfurling around me appeared to be built on a rocky foundation of superficiality and shallowness, and, whilst I don't think I was particularly disliked by anybody at school, I felt myself being quickly disregarded as potential friend material by most on the basis of my attitudes towards school (generally positive!), my choice of schoolbag, and the things I liked doing in my spare time. Very quickly, I was dubbed as a 'nerd' and 'too nice'—things that I would now view as a massive compliment (intelligent *and* kind; I'll take that!)—, but of course felt like the end of the world to an 11-year-old girl who, at the time, just wanted to be liked and accepted.

I also found the pacing of mainstream school to be incredibly frustrating: whilst I excelled at certain subjects (namely English and Religious Studies) and found my lessons just didn't quench my hunger for the depth I wished to go to with these subjects, I conversely massively struggled with others (Science and Geography, I'm talking about you!), simply because they *just didn't click* immediately—and, as a result of the rigid classroom structure—always abiding by someone else's deadline—, I fell behind on these subjects very quickly, and catching up quickly felt like an impossibility. It always felt like I was experiencing some extreme or another—either under-stimulation or complete overwhelm—, and this feeling didn't appear to be fading anytime soon.

In terms of my more personal issues, I started to endure some extreme bouts of anxiety: my mum had, less than two years before, left a very domestically violent relationship that had become normality for a good five years or so of my childhood—and it was, strangely enough, *after* this event that my mental health started to plummet. Whilst school had before been a safe haven away from the ever-worsening conflict at home during my primary school days, it was when all was over and the dust was settled that the reality of what our little family had endured began to crash over my shoulders, and I suddenly found myself having multiple panic attacks a day—the majority of which occurring before 9am—just at the thought of leaving my mum alone at home. In that panic-filled, irrational part of my brain, it felt like leaving my mum alone was a disaster waiting to happen, and this was something I struggled to cope with.

I believe it was as a result of a combination of feeling inadequate in certain subjects (thanks to the pacing of the lessons) and trying to reclaim some element of control over my life amidst the anxiety-riddled, irrational thoughts that seemed to penetrate my consciousness 24/7 that I quickly spiralled into some very obsessive, controlling behaviours surrounding my schoolwork—behaviours I was admired and congratulated for by my teachers and family members, since they reaped my desired results, but were ultimately driven by all the wrong reasons: a soul-crushing fear of failure, and, by the same token, losing control of the direction of my life again. I quickly propelled myself into overwork and extreme perfectionism, and something as seemingly harmless as losing a mark on a test paper, or being lightly scolded by a teacher for having the top button of my school shirt undone, would trigger a wave of self-hatred and panic.

It was around this time that I began to go to therapy sessions weekly—mainly for the after-effects of the domestic violence, but also for the anxiety I was experiencing at the time—and, whilst these therapy sessions did help somewhat in terms of my coming to terms with the past and rationalising these fears surrounding leaving my mum alone during the day, my anxiety just would not subside: I had now begun to associate school with these feelings of inadequacy and inner-turmoil and, soon enough, my anxiety became less about my fears surrounding my mum's safety and more about being on school grounds, period.

It was whilst on the way to school in around March 2015—six months after my joining secondary school—that I brought up the topic of home-schooling with my mum. Whilst part of me really did hope she would consider this as an option, the idea even to me felt like something far away, something intangible, a whisper of something that *could* be but that I couldn't visualise at all: I had been home-schooled for some of Year 5 two years before after myself and my family had moved to France, but this had been for a very short period of time, and we hadn't been following any specific format—my studies mostly consisted of reading classics, learning French with the locals, and plodding through some Maths textbooks. Other than this, I had no experience whatsoever with the notion of home-schooling. This meant that as much as I was desperate for an alternative solution to the draining day-to-day slog I currently felt I was in, the concept of home education was one that felt utterly alien and out of the question.

This, however, didn't seem to be the opinion my mum held towards the matter: she had, of course, been there to witness my transition from a confident—albeit shy—little girl to one filled with anxiety, overwhelm, obsessiveness, and slowly deteriorating self-esteem, and as a result, I think she was just as—if not more—desperate for me to find my happiness again—and school was very clearly the last thing facilitating this.

Even putting this emotional aspect to the side, I think my mum could also see that I just simply *wasn't reaching my potential*—and, sadly, this is the case for a wealth of perfectly capable students across the world who feel confined by the monotonousness of the mainstream schooling system. During my younger years, I would pore through encyclopaedias, Wikipedia pages, and YouTube, constantly on the hunt for knowledge—and now, my brain felt overwhelmed by random facts and figures that didn't seem to connect to a bigger picture in any way. School was less about education and more about being able to store enough random fragments of meaningless information in my short-term memory in order to pass the next test.

My mum told me to leave it with her, and the conversation was left.

It was a little over a month later, on a bright, cold Monday morning in April, that all of that changed. My mum was driving me to school, and I was breathing my way through my second panic attack of the morning: I had a French speaking test, and traffic was at a standstill—meaning I would probably be late to school and miss some of the assessment. This—predictably—had caused my anxiety to skyrocket, and it was as my mum was about to pull into the school that she stopped, turned the car around, and drove in the opposite direction.

'You're not going back there again,' she said simply, and the decision was made—and, in turn, my home-schooling journey commenced.

To this day, I don't think I have ever felt relief quite like I did in that moment: it was quite literally like the weight of the world had been removed from my shoulders. A fog I hadn't realised had been clouding my mind seemed to instantly evaporate, and whilst I had before regarded my immediate future with a kind of numb acceptance, it now felt like I had the world lying at my feet: it was a new chapter—one I could finally actually control the direction of.

The journey that commenced was by no means straightforward; in actuality, I would say I probably spent a good two years from that point simply trying to navigate *how* to home-school myself—that is, what resources to use, how I should go about putting goals in place, how actually to revise... The works. Whilst this was certainly not time wasted and the life skills I learned over this period—both academic and not—have benefitted me endlessly every day since (no exaggeration!), it is because of such a period that the purpose of this guide was born: so that *you* don't have to spend that time navigating the intricacies of home-schooling. Instead, I am going to be the helping hand to you that I wanted so badly during those initial years of home-schooling.

Looking back now, this period feels pretty funny to reflect on; whilst they may have felt impossible at the time, navigating these initial mistakes is, funnily enough, what I now specialise in helping others to overcome—proof that there is always a light at the end of the tunnel! As you'll see later, it was mainly by learning how to schedule my time *properly* and effectively (through trial-and-error!) that I *finally* managed to pull myself out of this initial panic-filled slump. Unfortunately (but also fortunately), it took a good few years of being at the extreme end of the scale (otherwise known as Extreme Overwork!) and hugely burning out as a result for me to realise such a schedule wasn't sustainable—and, hence, my current schedule was born. You can access this in the following link so you can get a better idea from the get-go of the kind of setup you may end up creating for yourself by the end of this book:

https://www.fayepaige.co/readersfreebie.

This is the schedule that I still use today, and has ultimately facilitated my achieving some of my biggest goals during my home-schooling journey.

Implement the lessons that follow actively, head on over to any of the resources that I mention if they pique your interest (they're only there for your benefit, after all!), and I promise both your academic pursuits and your overall attitude to education will take a massive turn. This guide is an ode to self-discipline, fruitful, enriching learning, and taking control of the direction of your own life.

Faye x

IS HOME-SCHOOLING RIGHT FOR YOU?

What Even Is Home-School?

BEFORE WE DELVE INTO the misconceptions, pros and cons, and what I, personally, feel I took from my years of home-education—the good and the bad!—, it seems that a good place to start when deciding whether home-schooling is a viable option for you (or your child) is actually establishing what we mean when we refer to 'home-school'.

The official definition for home-school is:

(verb): To educate [one's child] at home instead of sending them to school.

This may seem like a pretty straightforward definition—and, indeed, you probably have your own ideas already of what you imagine a typical home-school setup looks like—, but what actually is it to 'educate at home'? Is this definition even accurate?

Our loose answer to this is 'no'—mainly due to our glaring issue of the fact that home-school is defined as always occurring 'at home'. This is not always the case, nor would it be the case that at school all your learning would occur on-campus: there are also trips and at-home studying to consider.

Oftentimes, a reason people opt for home-education is their belief that learning should occur 'out in the real world', i.e., not at the confines of a desk, and, thus, a lot of people choose to learn by *experiences* rather than *the theories of those experiences* (e.g., going to a museum rather than learning a certain point in history from a textbook). We'll explore the different methods, if you will, of home-schooling in the next section, but for now, we can see just from this one example that active education and learning won't always take place in the home environment.

There is also nothing to stop a home-schooler from going out to a café or somewhere similar to complete their day's work—automatically refuting this definition's validity!

Note: The reason why we have to be so clear on this distinction between the definition of home-school and the reality of home-school is so that we can start to grasp quite how misunderstood the concept (and the image linked with) home-school usually is. If you have a specific image in your mind concerning what you believe all home-schooling constitutes, this is automatically incorrect—because there is no one set way to home-educate (which is kind of the point!).

So how actually can we define home-school? We'd still have to keep our new definition pretty vague (after all, every home-schooling experience completely varies from person-to-person—a point you'll see me stressing a lot in this book!), but I think home-school can be more suitably defined as:

(verb): To educate [oneself or one's child] independently and outside of the school environment.

This definition isn't perfect, but it gives us something to work with!

Misconceptions

Whenever it comes up in conversation that I spent the vast majority of my secondary school career home-educated (which is usually a daily occurrence, believe it or not!), reactions tend to follow a similar sequence:

- **Surprise** *('Wow, really?')*
- **A Remark** *('I would have loved that/I would have hated that')*
- **Questions, questions, questions.**

It's the latter stage we will now be focusing on here, as it is also during this point in the conversation that all of the person's preconceived assumptions and misconceptions about home-school arise. These are also probably (hopefully!) the main questions you, as the reader, may have about home-school. Some of these will be explored in much more detail later on, so don't worry if not all your questions get properly answered here; this is just a quick summary of the things you should know about before making a solid decision on whether home-school is for you.

You have to have a parent/guardian who is a teacher in order to be home-schooled. This is usually one of the first assumptions that come my way when the conversation of home-education comes up with someone, and it is (as you may be happy to hear!) completely untrue. There certainly are a lot of parents out there who are/were teachers and thus feel confident in teaching their children at home, but home-school is not limited to those who have relatives with experience in teaching. As touched on above, there are loads of ways of approaching home-schooling, and a lot of them don't involve any real-life teacher/tutor-to-student teaching whatsoever.

Home-schoolers are socially deprived and lack social skills. Besides the initial shock of 'going against the grain', the real confusion in terms of home-schooling seems to begin with how a child can possibly get the 'full social experience' they need in order to flourish without the social crutch of full-time public education. However, I find that the majority of home-schoolers actually lead a *healthier* (and, yes, still balanced) social life: they get to choose who they spend their time with and in what situation, leading to stronger, more valuable relationships—unlike in school, where they are forced to mix with potentially unsavoury characters that will hinder their personal growth. Things like bullying, damaging trends, peer pressure, etc. can be evaded completely, leading to higher self-esteem, improved mental health, and more focus in studies, within home-schooling. Of course, this will differ from person-to-person (as I touched on above, not every person is suited to home-education, and that's okay). It's about knowing how you work best and what you prioritise.

All home-schoolers are highly un/intelligent. People's views—or, shall we say, assumptions—tend to be at one extreme or the other when it comes to the intelligence to be expected from someone who is/was home-schooled: they either have an image of an Einstein-esque genius who is a complete jack-of-all-trades, or somebody highly unintelligent who simply wasn't cut out for the demands of a mainstream curriculum. A theme you may be noticing here in terms of the assumptions made about home-school is that home-schoolers are all perceived as being fundamentally different from all other people—after all, that'd make sense considering they're doing something fundamentally different from most other people their age, right?—, when in reality, home-schoolers are the same as anyone else—so, of course, intelligence levels will vary on an individual basis, in exactly the same way as they would in a school setting. It's true that home-schoolers may, perhaps, enjoy the schoolwork they are engaging in more so than when they were at school (thus fulfilling their potential more and coming across as more academic), but this could easily be the case for a schoolchild who thrives more than others in the mainstream schooling environment. It completely depends on the person at hand and their setup.

Home-schoolers do everything/nothing. Yet another assumption that sounds very extreme, but is also quite understandable. On the one hand, the only types of home-schoolers who are portrayed in the media tend to be those from wealthy backgrounds who (coupled with their superhuman intelligence, of course), can horse-ride, beat a professional player at chess, and speak three languages fluently by age eight, becoming a member of Mensa and securing their place in Oxbridge before they hit adolescence. On the other hand, we have the idea that if home-schoolers don't spend their days going to school, they mustn't do anything at *all*. This is where the stereotype of home-schoolers being 'drop-outs' also comes in, which can, quite frankly, be rather harmful, leading to a lot of people not even considering home-school in the first place (for themselves or their children) due to the stigma. We'll go into more detail over what a home-schooler's typical routine may comprise of later (or, as mentioned in our **Author's Note** section, you can access my very own personal schedule here:

https://www.fayepaige.co/readersfreebie

This will allow you to gain more of an intuition for this, but, as I'm sure you may have guessed by this point, neither extreme of opinion is always the case. Home-education is whatever you make it, and there are just as many—if not more—things to do and learn within home-school as there are within the school system.

Home-schooling is highly expensive. Besides concerns regarding their child's wellbeing, this is one of the first concerns parents tend to have concerning home-school—and, in my experience, one of the main reasons a lot of children never bring up the prospect of home-school with their parents. The idea that home-schooling is extortionate and thus out of the question for any families below the middle- and upper-class is, all things considered, an understandable assumption to make and, due to the significance of such a concern, we'll be going into this into much more depth later. For now, I can confidently say that a typical home-schooling experience will *never* be more expensive than public schooling (unless you are enrolling your child in those horse-riding and chess masterclasses; then I'd say your concerns are very valid!). This may seem very counterintuitive as, at least here in the UK, all pre-university education is completely free, including all the resources and facilities required. However, what we neglect to take into consideration is all the little things required to facilitate our children going to school: schoolbags, school uniform, packed lunches, school trips, transport to and from school, 'Non-School Uniform Day'... the list goes on. And that's without mentioning the *indirect* monetary pressures placed on parents resulting from school (i.e., that bag you/your child *must have* so as to avoid being the butt of the classroom's jokes). Still not convinced? Worry not; I'll be comprehensively breaking down the typical costs involved in home-education compared with that of mainstream education later on, and you'll see there's nothing to worry about!

Home-schoolers 'miss out'. Believe it or not, one of the first reactions I got from my peers when I left school for home-education was, 'But you're going to miss *prom!*' As much as this sounded ridiculous to 11-year-old-Faye at the time—fancy staying and being miserable in school for five years just so I can put on a pretty dress at the end of it!—, this actually had some merit: after all, as much as secondary school (and college/Sixth Form) are acknowledged by most as not being the easiest time you'll ever have in your life, most hold a good handful of their memories derived from these times close—memories from the classroom, from school trips, from evenings out with friends, from particular classes and teachers—, memories they feel could never be replicated from outside the classroom. This is completely valid, but then again, we need to think: if the behind-the-scenes of our school setup makes us miserable, should we really stay just for the highlight reel? Are moments such as prom, leavers', nights out, and the odd happy snippet from a particularly good lesson or meet-up, going to balance out the dread some of us feel going into school every day? What about when bullying, social isolation, and extreme exam stress come into play? These are the things that require real thought when making a decision about home-schooling, and will help to differentiate between those suited to home-school and those not.

You have to adhere to the GCSE/A-Level curricula when doing home-school. The answer to this one is very simple: it depends on whether you're sitting these external exams or not (which, by the way, are completely optional). If you're sitting these exams then, of course, you'll want to follow such curricula in order to pass the exams (I will cover the ways in which you can do this in our section concerning the methods of home-school, as will how you would go about sitting exams). Don't think, however, that if you *are* sitting these exams then this is the only curriculum you can follow— you can still pursue your other interests alongside learning for your exams! If you're not sitting exams, however, then you are, from a legal standpoint, allowed to do whatever you like, so long as you are still being educated. (But we'll go further into the legalities—or, rather, lack thereof!—of home-schooling later.)

Home-schoolers struggle to get into work/further education. Now, as much as home-school brings flexibility and more scope into a student's life and routine, there should, of course, be an element of long-term planning in order for this concern/misconception not being brought into fruition. As mentioned above, home-school is what you make it, and you will reap the benefits from the effort you put into it—and, by the same token, home-schoolers will be at a disadvantage if things aren't planned for properly. **For example:** If you know you/your child is/are planning on going into the medical field, then there will, of course, be exams, work experience, and entry requirements (whether that be into a university or a career) to be considered—as is the case for when they are in public education. The difference here is that home-school may actually allow for more opportunity for a unique application into such things (e.g., alternative, higher-level qualifications; tangible life experience in such sectors)—it's just about doing the research and putting in that extra effort.

Of course, there are far more—perhaps even endless amounts of—assumptions we could tackle here, but the above lays a good foundation in terms of what we should and shouldn't expect from home-education—and, hopefully, clears up some fundamental misconceptions we most certainly *don't* want to be carrying when weighing up home-education. Home-schooling is not limited to those with good connections and an unusually high IQ, nor does it lead to social incompetence, lack of social experience, laziness, and/or unemployment. Home-education is a viable option for everyone, and oftentimes leads to the development of some real, tangible skills and characteristics those within the restraints of a classroom are unlikely to obtain.

The Pros and Cons of Home-Schooling

Now that we have cleared up the most common misconceptions of home-education, let us weigh up the positives and negatives of home-schooling. **Please bear in mind this is all very subjective**; something I may view as a negative, you may view as a positive, and vice-versa.

Pros
Complete freedom of expression. This may seem like it wouldn't be a particularly relevant element of home-education—nor is it something you may be considering when

evaluating whether home-school is for you. However, I can honestly say that, when reflecting on my years of home-schooling, this was by far the biggest benefit, and has—cheesy as it sounds!—completely changed me as a person for the better—hence why it is, for me, at the top of this list. Things as seemingly trivial as feeling able to wear what I liked and listen to the music that I wanted without fear of judgement made a world of difference and made me feel as though I was being authentic to myself. This has resulted in me just being *more comfortable in me.* This also stretched to more serious topics, such as coming out as bisexual and being open about when my mental health was suffering. I had spent enough time with myself to know that I was fine the way I was, that I didn't need to change, and that expressing myself was okay.

Control across the board. From the content you learn and how you learn it, to the people you surround yourself with, to the time you choose to wake up in the morning, you are in control of pretty much *every decision you make on a daily basis.* This can be both overwhelming and amazing, and was one of my favourite things about home-schooling. If the weather was beautiful, I could sit outside and be just as productive; if I felt unmotivated and unfocused, I could take a break, switch up my content, or continue my pursuits in a café, library, bookstore, art gallery, or wherever struck my fancy. I could prioritise subjects outside of my secondary school's GCSE curricula that sparked excitement and interest—philosophy, psychology, astronomy—rather than slaving over a subject I wouldn't touch again after my GCSEs.

In summary, I feel I was able to fulfil my academic potential at the same time as I was able to fuel my lust for life—something I lost very quickly within the constraints of a classroom.

Time (and more of an appreciation for it). This was probably one of the strangest adjustments I felt when I began home-school: I had been used to virtually every hour of my day being booked up with something, my life governed by timetables—and now, it felt like I had nothing but time. Exploiting the time now at your disposal can be a matter of huge overwhelm for newbie home-schoolers—something that is super understandable, but is something that, when nipped in the bud ASAP, guarantees some *insane* results in a matter of days. I offer more guidance into this at https://www.fayepaige.co/readersfreebie, since this is where the true gold lies but is often difficult to master when you have no previous experience of time-management in home-schooling. Indeed, it was with the formation of such a sustainable and consistent routine that I found myself able to put my spare time (and there was a lot of it!) into good use: suddenly, I had the time to do all the things I had promised myself I would do, but had never gotten round to doing, such as learning French (*properly* this time), running, learning to play guitar, and reading classic literature. As a result of this, I like to consider myself to be a fairly well-rounded and self-aware person—and this is all because I not only had enough hours in the day to focus on what was important to me, but I began to understand *quite how much* could be fit into those precious hours—all with some simple time-management strategies!

Self-Care. This links nicely to the idea of home-school providing you with more time, as I also found that this time allowed for me to take care of me: I took up journaling, meditation, and started paying more attention to my diet and the thoughts I was putting out into the world. I started waking up at 4:30am every morning (yes, even on the weekend!) because I was at my happiest when I could watch the sunrise and kickstart the day with some me-time. When you spend so much time with yourself, you start noticing things about yourself and your current habits—both good and bad—that you perhaps wouldn't have realised before and, because you have the **time** and **control** at your disposal, you are actually able to dedicate time to self-improvement and the things that bring you happiness—whether that be travelling, painting, gaming, or reading. **You basically become your own Number One Priority**—a stark contrast to the 'hustle culture' take on self-care, whereby adhering to a school timetable is of higher importance than your personal needs and wants.

Enhanced academic performance. Of course, this isn't always guaranteed with home-school—a setup requiring minimum effort for the home-schooler is never going to breed the next Hawking—but, assuming the necessary effort is put in and that an effective scheduling approach is implemented, there is a very fair chance that a given home-schooler will find themselves engaging more in their schoolwork, simply because they are more suited to the learning style and thus enjoy it more. There is also arguably a wider scope of study, depending on the approach taken to home-school (as lightly touched on above); whilst most primary school students are limited to the fundamentals of Maths, English, and Science, home-schoolers have the option to explore whatever piques their interest.

Cons

The transition. Whilst this element of home-education is temporary, some actually struggle more than you would expect with the transition from mainstream education to home-schooling. After all, this is a **major lifestyle change**—a change that comes with a lot of responsibility—that can mean the pace of your entire household shifts. This feeling isn't always inevitable: some breeze through the transition and quickly feel in their element. However, I think it's fair to say that, for the most part, the transition can be a little overwhelming at times—and that's okay! With the formation of balanced, sustainable habits and routine, things will fall into place.

The initial financial shock. As mentioned above, we will go into the finances of home-schooling a little later in this book; and, like also mentioned above, home-schooling is not nearly as financially demanding as most people would think. However, **the setting-up of home-schooling can be fairly expensive.** Indeed, with public schooling, costs are kind of spread evenly throughout the school year: new school uniform at the beginning; school trip midway through the year; £15 each week on school lunches. With home-schooling, on the other hand, you'll find that **most of the things needed throughout the year will need to be bought from the get-go.** This will be the case for any online courses you enrol in, any tutors (if wanted/needed), and basic resources, such as stationery and textbooks. The good news is that (as mentioned in our **Misconceptions** section), you'll most likely end up altogether spending way less on home-school than you would for public school—it's just that it tends to be in bigger chunks at a time rather than small bits here and there.

Responsibility and resilience. I would say this is the factor that separates those who would thrive within home-education and those who would struggle a little more—and, in turn, I would say is the number one thing that needs weighing up as objectively as possible. **Home-education**—no matter what the approach to it you take—**takes willpower.** It is—I would say inarguably—less convenient than public schooling, and requires active planning, engagement, and consistency. This doesn't mean you have to do the exact same thing every day—switching up the content you're learning and how you learn it is something I would actually recommend, and is one of the best parts of home-education—, but there are some underlying elements of home-schooling that should **always** remain constant in order for home-education to be **productive and sustainable** (but more on this later)—and these elements require an adequate amount of self-motivation.

Schooling slumps. This happens to the best of us—not just in terms of schooling, but across the board. We head into a new stage of our lives, a new decision, a new hobby, a new task, and a few days, weeks, months into our endeavours, we burn out—and that's okay. The difference in terms of academia, however, is that when we burn out in school, we have **external reinforcers all around us**: teachers willing for us to get that next grade; friends who are in the same boat... Even the change of scene of school when we're used to being at home can pull us out of a funk. When you're home-schooled, on the other hand, you are, for the most part, **your own primary champion**—meaning (as also mentioned above) a lot of self-motivation is needed in order for you to get the best experience from home-schooling. This doesn't mean that these slumps won't happen anymore, but it does mean you'll be better equipped to pull yourself *out* of those slumps and get back on track.

Being different. Now, this one is very much so a bit of a grey area, and a lot of people (myself included, for the most part) would say being different is a good thing—and, indeed, it does certainly open up room for conversation, and will inevitably give you a skillset most people will spend their whole lives developing. Upon reflection, I have absolutely no hang-ups over the fact that I did something different to everyone else I knew in terms of my education, and there are actually a ton of examples of times I was actually able to work this difference to my advantage. However, I would be lying if I said that, at times, being different felt a little tough—not in terms of the tangible consequences, but in terms of **having people to relate to** and, occasionally, feelings of **missing out**. Now, this is the one con of home-schooling on this list that I would actually advise readers not to dwell on too much: the positives of home-education—as well as how easy, with the right mindset, the majority of the cons are to overcome— massively outweigh the drawback of the occasional feeling of FOMO. Saying this, I do still feel it's relevant to put this on this list: I have zero regrets over home-schooling, and I find that, generally speaking, I reflect upon my secondary school years during home-education with far more happiness than those who were in public schooling—but, there were times I really missed the social buzz of classes, the connections I developed with teachers, and partaking in specific special events (e.g., the beginning and end of the school year; leavers'; school trips). However, please refer back to what we spoke about in our **Misconceptions** section in regard to 'home-schoolers missing out'—i.e., that we can comfortably conclude that they overall *don't* miss out. However, **it can feel that way**—especially with social media only showing the positives of a given person's life. Nonetheless, this is not something to worry about as these feelings will, in my experience, always be short-lived as you continue to thrive in your home-schooling setup.

So, there you have it: my own (very subjective but, debatably, valuable!) take on what I feel are the positives and negatives of home-education. Of course, you should take all of the above with a pinch of salt: this is going off my own personal experience of being home-schooled for (as I'm writing this) five years (with probably around four more to go!). Your own list (if you choose home-education is the avenue for you) will undoubtedly differ—perhaps significantly so—from mine. Nonetheless, the above hopefully provides some food for thought, and a loose indication of the sort of things that can be expected from home-schooling.

Home-Schooling Skillsets: What is Needed and What is Developed

It seems fitting to close this introduction to home-education with an ode to the skills I feel I developed (and that you would likely develop!) over the course of home-education—as well as the skills/traits I already had that massively came in handy when getting into the swing of home-schooling. Again, this can be viewed as a rough guide: if you know you already have these skills to an extent, then you're off to an amazing start—and if you don't, then this is a good framework to go off in terms of how to hone your skills and mindset so as to fulfil your potential, whether that be in terms of academics, your social life, or your overall day-to-day lifestyle, during your home-schooling years.

The self-setting and actualising of goals. Now, goal-setting is one of the first things a lot of us are taught to do in school—and yet how much does the typical school actually encourage this? What a great deal of us already acknowledge is that school tends to set the main bulk of our goals—at least in terms of academics—for us, and it's because of this that we tend to see the majority of students outside (and, in some cases, even inside) the school setting completely lacking the skill of goal-setting—some of us even carrying this struggle into adulthood. This can be seen when we claim we're going to start frequently going to the gym, eating healthily, seriously learning a language, spending less time on our phones, sorting out our sleep cycles... The list goes on and on. This may seem unrelated to home-schooling, but we've got to remember to actually look at the bigger picture when evaluating home-education: during any given day of home-schooling, regardless of the approach you are taking, you constantly have to set goals, and **be invested enough in yourself in terms of achieving them to actually do so**. After all, there's no register with your name on it waiting to be ticked off at a specific place and time; everything you will ever do over the course of home-education will have to entirely come from a place of self-motivation in terms of your goals because **you want to achieve** and because **you are invested in them and their tangible outcomes**. Home-schooling also, of course, encourages the practical aspect of goals (not just the habit of setting them): actualising goals becomes a skill you're almost forced to learn during home-schooling, simply because of the self-reliant nature of it. Suddenly, learning chemistry isn't as simple as turning up to a chemistry class: your overall goal has to be broken down into bite-sized chunks in terms of what units you'll learn this week and how you will learn them.

The ability to adhere to a routine. The overall idea of a routine may sound rather contradictory to the idea of home-school: isn't home-schooling supposed to be a break *away* from routine? Isn't it the restrictive nature of routine that tends to staunch development, both personal and academic? The answer to this is yes and no; yes because the routine adopted in *schools* (usually in the form of timetables) almost always prioritises not the students and them learning the best, but what is cheapest and most convenient. However, not all routines are like this and, when formed with you as the priority, routine generally **enhances efficiency**, **reduces time wastage**, **makes us feel more in control of our lives**... the list goes on. We'll be going into a lot of detail about routine and how you should incorporate it into your home-schooling later so you're not completely adrift on a daily basis—but for now, just know that routine *is and should be* an integral part of your daily home-schooling routine. This is a skill that will allow you to get into positive habits, make advanced, forward-thinking decisions, and feel more fulfilled as a person **for the rest of your life**—guaranteed.

Self-discipline. Yet another skill most struggle with throughout the course of their lives that is at the core of almost every single home-schooling experience out there— and is, for me personally, I think my biggest takeaway from home-education. There is something ridiculously fulfilling about being able to **trust yourself to take care of yourself**

and to **act in your own best interests**. Indeed, it's no secret that humans, in their very nature, tend to be quite self-sabotaging: we are procrastinators, overthinkers, and don't like to be predicted, so we often go above and beyond to avoid what we know we should be doing—usually shooting ourselves in the foot in the process. However, when you fall into the world of home-education and are suddenly held accountable for every decision you make—not by somebody who means nothing to you, but by *yourself*—, the development of self-discipline becomes far more achievable.

Independence. This one is pretty self-explanatory, and is often one of the main appeals of home-schooling. Indeed, as much as it may *seem* like schools encourage independence in their students (especially in Year 11, when GCSEs are looming, and from that point onward as students approach adulthood), even this is only encouraged in terms of being **reactive** rather than **proactive**. Things like being punctual to lessons and deadlines are certainly very good traits to have, but it's when we're **not under pressure to respond to a deadline** that our independence is truly put to the test—and this is, of course, the backbone of home-schooling; thus, we can say that the establishing, developing, and maintaining of independence is also the backbone of home-schooling. As you may also expect, this independence also very much so gets carried outside the schooling side of things: for me personally, I've found I feel way more confident in terms of my problem-solving skills as a result of this independence I've formed. If something isn't going well—from a technical issue on my laptop, to navigating public transport alone, to pinpointing bad habits I'm getting into that are taking a negative toll on my life—, I automatically reason my way through it rather than automatically seeking my mum's help. Of course, I still know I *can* ask for help if needed, but as your confidence in yourself grows and you become more resilient and independent in the face of inconvenience and conflict, you find yourself needing this help less and less.

Now that we are better acquainted with the notion of home-schooling, what it entails, its advantages and disadvantages, and the skills we can generally expect to obtain from home-schooling (when done properly, of course), you should hopefully have a more solid, informed idea of whether home-schooling would be right for you/your child(ren)—and not only that, but for this time in your life.

As much as from the above it may seem like I am rather biased toward home-schooling, home-schooling varies massively, as I keep stressing—not just from person-to-person, but also from experience-to-experience. For example, as I briefly mentioned in our **Author's Note** section, I was home-schooled for a (very short) period of time in Year 5, when my family and I moved to France for just shy of a year. I enjoyed my home-schooling there but re-joined school pretty much as soon as we landed back in the UK as **that was where I knew I was meant to be**. That doesn't mean my home-schooling during that time was bad, or that I spent the whole time yearning for school, or that I wasn't cut out for home-education; I just knew that, at that time, public school was the place for me—and it so happened to continue to be for the remainder of my time in primary school.

Similarly, I knew pretty quickly that secondary school wasn't for me—whereas home-schooling during *this* time **just felt right**. This won't always be the case for every person—as mentioned above, the transition period can be difficult considering the huge change in lifestyle it entails—, but once things settle down, I think it becomes pretty evident very quickly whether we are suited to home-schooling or not—as people, and at this place in our lives.

Home-schooling isn't set in stone. If you decide after a few weeks, months, or years that it isn't for you, or that there's some other public avenue you would like to explore, that's entirely your decision. Remember, **this life is yours**, so do what you want with it; you're only doing yourself a disservice by doing otherwise.

This is, indeed, one of my main reasons for writing this book: after all, home-school is stigmatised in so many ways, and is as a result often considered to be a strange, rebellious, and risky alternative to public schooling—when in reality, most of us would probably find we were/will be more suited to home-education at a certain point in our lives.

Let's normalise home-schooling as the valid, promising route to take for education that it is!

WHAT ARE THE DIFFERENT ROUTES OF HOME-SCHOOLING?

NOW THAT WE HAVE looked over some of the **whys** of home-schooling, lets delve into what seems to be the biggest question mark hanging over home-schooling: **how**?

Whack this question into Google and you'll get over **42 million** results. You'll also get some pretty intimidating statistics in terms of the amount of people who are currently home-schooling: according to the National Centre for Education Statistics (NCES), as of 2012, **1.8 million** children were being home-schooled (3.4% of the total student population!)—and this is thought to have increased by **40% in the last three years** (although there are no recent studies for this).

So, if so many people are home-schooling, how are they actually doing it?

This is a little difficult to summarise or put into list form considering—say it with me—every home-schooling experience is different. However, I would say there are four types, if you will, of home-schooling that are commonly adopted in the UK.

The National Curriculum

The first option—and, perhaps, the most intuitive one—is to simply adhere to the national curriculum. I would say this one is the 'safest' option: parents/home-schoolers essentially have a pre-set to-do list with this approach, incorporating everything their peers will also be doing in mainstream education.

How?: This is surprisingly a little-known fact, but a complete breakdown of the national curriculum is available on www.gov.uk, including *what* is taught (i.e., what units will be covered) and *why* these things are taught. Do be warned, the first time looking up this curriculum can be a little overwhelming to someone who has no experience in teaching considering its depth, but I promise all of it is actually surprisingly easy to wrap your head around, no matter what the level of education you are looking into.

Resources: You have access to pretty much every resource a teacher does, including websites, videos, textbooks, past papers—and these resources are *super* easy to find if you're simply adhering to the national curriculum. Enter 'Key Stage 2 Science' into Google and boom: streams of textbooks, articles, and videos, all with everything you/your child would have learnt in school and more.

Please bear in mind that if you are studying content specifically in mind of exams (e.g., GCSEs; A-Levels), you'll need to adhere to a specific exam board's curriculum (which can be found on their respective websites), as these can vary in terms of content. **For example:** If you're sitting your

English GCSE with AQA, you'll want to look up AQA's specification and also possibly buy an AQA English textbook; similarly, if you're sitting GCSE Maths with Edexcel, you'll want to buy their corresponding textbook(s) and cover everything on their specification. (But we'll go more into the specifics of booking and sitting exams later.)

You can also buy online courses named Distance Learning Platforms that will literally teach you everything you'll need to know for any GCSE/A-Level curriculum. These can be fairly expensive, but a lot of home-schoolers find this worth it in terms of the confidence (as it's not like you will end up accidentally skipping past a key part of the curriculum) and the convenience it provides. Some websites that provide this are ICS, NCC Home-Learning, and NEC. (But more on these later.)

Advantages: The clear advantage of this approach is that you never run the risk of falling behind your peers; you're learning exactly what they are, only with a pace more tailored to you. This can mean this approach is very reassuring, and it also paves the way for you sitting exams if you wish to. This also upkeeps an element of structure in your/your child's life, as you're not taking on a silly amount of work whilst still keeping busy.

Disadvantages: One of my favourite parts about home-schooling was that I was able to explore subjects and topics **outside of the national curriculum** (some of which being ancient history, philosophy, and criminology, none of which I have ever heard of being on a GCSE curriculum). It was the exploration of such subjects that allowed me to actually figure out what I find interesting and, in turn, what I want to pursue in the future. Indeed, there are a lot of arguments saying the national curriculum is restrictive and does not encourage creativity or curiosity. Leading from this, I would also say it's far more likely learners will go through **learning slumps** (which we tackled in **our Cons of Home-Schooling** section), as these subjects have not been chosen from a place of genuine interest, but from a feeling of necessity—leading to the studying of such subjects often feeling monotonous and pointless.

My Recommendations: A reoccurring theme you'll find as we go through the methods of home-schooling is my recommending of a *combination* of these methods, rather than just sticking to one approach religiously, and this is most certainly the case here. There is a lot to be said for following the national curriculum—it's been formulated by experts, after all—, and, when it comes to primary-school-age children, a lot of parents opt for using the curriculum for **core subjects** (e.g., English, maths, and science), which I think is a pretty sensible idea as most topics covered at that stage are central to our understanding of the world. However, this doesn't necessarily have to be done by poring through textbooks or filling out worksheets; you can get creative with this and do this in whatever way is best for you/your child. When it comes to Key Stage 3 and onwards, I would recommend you follow the national curriculum for English and maths, as well as for any GCSEs you want to be sitting (if any). Again, though, this doesn't have to be solely done through textbooks; watch videos, listen to podcasts, read books. **Interact with your subjects.**

The Charlotte Mason Method
This is a very commonly used approach in home-education, especially amongst younger home-schoolers.

This approach was formulated by—you guessed it— Charlotte Mason, who was an English educator whose philosophy basically centred around the idea that education should coach **not just the mind**, but the **whole person**. She based her method on the principle of education actually being made up of three factors: **Atmosphere** (i.e., the setting one both grows up in and receives their education in), **Discipline** (i.e., the establishment and maintaining of good habits), and **Life** (i.e., learning). The general idea was that that **content would be brought to life** for students, rather than them just being force-fed dry facts. There was no passively copying from a textbook, or test papers, involved in this method: instead, students would read books by those passionate about the subject at hand—and then would explain, in their own words, their own takes on what they had learnt, perhaps linking back to a personal past experience or to something else learnt in another topic.

Essentially, content and learning would be made **personal to them** through the constant formation of mental connections and incorporation of mental growth within their lessons.

A general misconception of the Charlotte Mason method is that only those who are religious implement this approach, as Mason placed a lot of emphasis on 'interacting with God's creation' and 'pointing the child towards God'; however, this element doesn't have to be incorporated—although you can certainly prioritise staying in touch with nature and your spirituality whilst using this approach, if this suits you better.

If you'd like to know more about this approach (as it's pretty intricate and takes a sort of intuition for it), I'd suggest having a read through the book *The Charlotte Mason Way Explained* by Dollie Freeman.

How?: As you may or may not have taken from the above summary, the ways in which the Charlotte Mason method is implemented vary greatly from case-to-case, in the sense that our opinions of what connotates 'personal growth' differ: for some, this could mainly centre on furthering religious beliefs; for others, it could be creating art and reading books; and for others, it could largely focus on an appreciation for nature and the Earth.

Either way, in order to kickstart your journey in the Charlotte Mason method, you will need two things: 1) the understanding that this is not a **curriculum** or a **step-by-step guide**, but a **method** whereby its underlying principles are outlined and the rest needs to be filled in by you; and 2) your own personal outline of what *you* feel is important within your/your child's daily routine—all, of course, in mind of personal growth and rich learning.

Still feeling adrift in terms of how you could implement the Charlotte Mason approach? Here are some of her recommendations:

1. **Living Books:** As touched on in the summary of this method, rather than students passively poring through textbooks, Mason implemented what she called *living books*— i.e., books written by those passionate about their subjects, such as poetry, autobiographies, and classical literature—, written in a conversational, friendly tone. Charlotte would read these *with* her students, and would then ask them to explain, in their own words, what they felt the book was trying to get across and what they have taken away from it. This, according to Charlotte, enriched their learning experience, making it **personal and applicable to them**.

2. **Short Lessons and Free Afternoons:** A particular issue in the mainstream schooling system at *any* given level of education—whether that be primary, secondary, college, or university— is lack of concentration, boredom, and fidgeting in students within the classroom. It is because of this that Charlotte employed short lessons and free afternoons for *all* students (although, notably, she would increase lesson time as her students grew older). By reducing the **quantity** of the time spent in-lesson, she—and her students—could fully focus on the **quality** of the learning being done. This, as you would expect, reduced boredom and restlessness and optimised attention span and optimism. Meanwhile, in their

free afternoons, students were urged to put their morning's learning into practice in whatever way they wanted to; either that, or to pursue a personal interest or hobby.

3. Habit Formation: Also touched on in our summary, the core philosophy behind Mason's method was to enrich the whole student, not just their mind, and she felt a massive part of this was down to the formation of good habits. These generally followed along the lines of obedience, attentiveness, and observation, and she claimed that the way in which a mother would attend to and care for her ill child should also be applied in equal measure to a child developing their good habits.

Resources: The point of the Charlotte Mason approach, as you may be gathering by this point, has been intentionally designed to accommodate for you/your child specifically; thus, the things you decide to incorporate in a timetable will vary from the next person implementing this method, thus making it difficult to pinpoint specific resources.

Saying this, there are some books that can provide some guidance for this method, including furthering your intuition for it and ideas of lessons. These are: *The Charlotte Mason Way Explained* by Dollie Freeman; *When Children Love to Learn: A Practical Application for Charlotte Mason's Philosophy Today* by Elaine Cooper; and *Charlotte Mason Study Guide* by Penny Gardner.

Other than these reads, I recommend you get creative with your resources and tailor your sources in mind of you/your child: watch videos, documentaries, and movies about your subjects; explore any literature produced by a leader in a specific field; and, if possible, interact with your learning as much as possible (e.g., actually visit a place of historical significance; conduct basic scientific experiments; explore geography directly, in nature). Meanwhile, in your free afternoons (if this is an aspect you choose to implement), research a topic of interest, learn to play an instrument you always wanted to, go on a hike, volunteer in your local community—literally anything you feel brings you happiness and personal growth.

Advantages: Personally, I think Mason hit the nail on the head in terms of what education should encompass and the ways in which this can be achieved: this balance of education and exploration has been tried and tested by home-schoolers worldwide and so far, they seem to be thriving. The interactivity this approach uses within active learning is also very valuable: making students *want* to learn and be interested in the content is, I think, the antidote to the **school slump** and general educational fatigue—and I think anybody who has undergone *any* form of education will be able to attest to this. If we don't think a topic applies or is of any interest to us, we switch off, and life becomes a lot more difficult; conversely, when we are invested and interested in a topic, we become more attentive and, thus, soak up information far more easily—and this is exactly what the Charlotte Mason method facilitates.

Disadvantages: It may seem from the above that this method is flawless and will undoubtedly produce the most well-educated and rounded people in the world, but, like with anything, there are both benefits and drawbacks to this approach. The main thing to bear in mind here is that this method was created **over 100 years ago**—and so, naturally, some aspects of her method, when left unadjusted, are pretty outdated. Not as many subjects were taught then as are now, the main priority of educators in those days being to make sure students were actually **numerate** and **literate**—i.e., could read and write. Of course, at least in Western culture, we no longer have this as our main priority, and tend to focus on the realms of science, humanities, language, and art rather early on. **This was not a part of the Charlotte Mason method**. Thus, whilst to some it may sound quite nice to learn most things through books and nature, this isn't always practical for all subjects—leaving this method in need of some adjustment.

Furthermore, this approach takes pretty consistent planning, and, considering the whole philosophy essentially relies on learners being **engaged**, this can be a little tiresome for not just pupils, but whoever is planning the learning (e.g., parents, carers, or the students themselves). However, you could argue that this is compensated by a) the short duration of the lessons and b) the time off it recommends. Essentially, it is up to you, the reader, to realistically determine whether the consistent planning and effort this approach necessitates is sustainable for you and your setup.

My Recommendations: From what I can gather, this method is most commonly implemented amongst parents who personally home-school their younger children, and I can see why: after all, one of the main questions parents of home-schoolers receive is simply *how do you get them to listen*, and this is quite easily answered by the simplicity and high quality of the Charlotte Mason method—which has, as we can see, clearly been formulated by Mason's own experience as an educator in terms of the psychology behind learning in children.

Indeed, when it comes to educating this age group in particular (i.e., primary school age), I would actually dub this as the 'best' approach (of course, take this loosely: this is my subjective opinion!). I am a massive advocate of **getting in touch with nature and yourself and gaining an intuition for your subjects** in order to get the best possible experience out of education (not just home-education!), and Mason seems to have understood this, too. It is because of this that I would recommend at least the general framework of this method being applied to all home-schooling routines (no matter what the age), with perhaps more of an emphasis on it during younger years (i.e., when habit and attitude formation is at its peak) to ensure long-term effective learning.

When it comes to older home-schoolers, however (I'd say from age 12 and above), whilst I still think the general idea of this approach should be implemented (i.e., tracking of habits, good and bad; ensuring learning is active and personal), I would say **shorter lessons** aren't as necessary. If you struggle with concentrating for long periods of time, I would strongly recommend the POMODORO Technique (i.e., 25 minutes of solid, uninterrupted work, followed by a five-minute total break, repeated four times before a longer break [e.g., 15-30 minutes] is taken), amongst other 'hacks', if you will, to longer concentration that we'll go into in a separate chapter. During these years, it's good and, ultimately, very important, I think, to get into the habit of doing longer bouts of work and practicing long-term gratification (especially if you're doing exams and have a spec to get through)—and I don't think this is fully facilitated for in the Charlotte Mason approach.

What I'm trying to get at here is that, as per, you should adjust every method to suit you personally, and the Charlotte Mason approach is no exception to this rule.

World Schooling

They say that 'the world is a classroom', and it is in World Schooling that this idea is taken very literally! World Schooling is generally implemented amongst those who view cultural immersion and travel as integral to a full learning experience; families/individuals will travel from place-to-place, the idea being that the landscapes, people, and cultures will teach you all you need to know for life. Nature is your teacher, and your curriculum is humanity.

How?: This is a rather liberal form of education—in other words, it's a relaxed, mostly student-led form of education. The umbrella term 'World Schooling' also includes those who travel and decide to enrol their children/themselves in schools as they go as a way to integrate in the culture further, but this, of course, is unrelated to the home-schooling branch of World Schooling we're concerned with, so we won't be going into any depth over this.

Individuals differ in terms of the approach they take the World Schooling: some still choose to follow the National Curriculum by bringing their resources with them from place to place, writing off their afternoons/evening for leisure and exploration in the community at hand, whilst others take an almost 'Unschooling' approach to it (see below), taking each day as it comes without any 'grander' objective in mind besides to explore, document, and widen their horizons.

Advantages: World Schooling is, in a lot of ways and for a lot of people, the ideal way of educating and living: it is **intuitive, fulfilling**, and lends the way to a whole scope of skills, such as empathy, an appreciation of different art and cultures, respect, curiosity, exploration, and leadership—which are, of course, highly impressive skills to be developing from a young age. It also adds **diversity** and **excitement** to a daily routine, and **pushes your boundaries**, whether that's by doing a particularly difficult hike, or by partaking in a gruelling conservation project. Overall, I think most would agree this approach to schooling is massively **character-building**, and develops a breadth of **life skills** that could not be learnt inside the classroom.

Disadvantages: The clearest disadvantage to this approach—and probably the main reason most don't utilise it—is the practical and monetary side to World Schooling: after all, it is no secret that most families can't afford to travel from place-to-place. Saying this, the financial element to World Schooling is not necessarily as simple as it being 'expensive': costs of living range massively from place to place (e.g., average rent in Honulu, Hawaii, is £3,000 a month, whereas that in Koh Samui, Thailand, is 10% of that at roughly £300 a month), and families frequently plan their travels in accordance with when flights, accommodation, etc. are cheaper. Thus, contrary to popular belief, World Schooling is not just reserved to the privileged; it is an option for most with a fairly consistent income and portable jobs.

The more valid argument against World Schooling is, of course, the issue of stability and consistency (especially when it comes to families of young children). This, of course, will differ from family-to-family in terms of whether this is a viable issue or not: for example, children (and adults) with autism tend to have a need for routine and balance, which could not be achieved when moving every month. On the other hand, travelling (whilst this may sound rather counterintuitive) has been found to alleviate symptoms of anxiety, so this may be a reason some families opt for World Schooling.

There is also, of course, the question of whether World Schooling (particularly when families/individuals choose not the follow a specific curriculum) actually lends the way to a well-rounded education. After all, students won't learn algebra and what an adjective is simply by climbing a mountain! Whilst this is a valid concern, it is here I would like to remind readers of the fact that **nothing with home-**

schooling is set in stone, and *everything* is flexible and open to change at any given time if needed. Thus, if you choose to implement World Schooling as your primary framework, this doesn't mean you're prohibited from picking up a chemistry textbook ever again. A lot of home-schooling is based on trial-and=error, so if something isn't working for you, there is nothing stopping you from mixing up your approach, taking something here and there from other popular home-schooling methods, and finding your happy medium.

My Recommendations: As briefly mentioned earlier in this book, I lived in France for a few months when I was nine, my family's original plan actually being to travel Europe, staying in each country for a few months, getting a taste of the culture and lifestyle in each place before moving onto the next. I was also home-schooled during this time, and so you could say, in a sense, I was World Schooled for that time: a lot of my studies were preoccupied with learning the language, drawing the new landscapes before me, and getting used to French culture and conversations—i.e., the new cultural aspects of my life.

Saying this, I also still upkept a few of my core subjects (namely English literature—it was at this time I discovered my love for *Little Women* by Louisa May Alcott—and maths), and it is this that I would recommend during World Schooling: cultural immersion, still with a loose sense of consistency in core subjects. I suppose my recommendations would be reminiscent of that of Charlotte Mason's in that way: a short but dedicated daily time space for sit-down academics, learning, and reflection; and the rest of the day allocated for implementation, questioning, and exploration— and, in the case of World Schooling specifically, culture.

Individual Courses/Subjects

This is the approach I, personally, followed over the course of my home-schooling years during secondary school, it being what its name suggests: the exploring of specific subjects that interest you at any given time. This is frequently implemented by those not sitting any exams as it allows for controlled exploration and learning, whilst still (as I would recommend) incorporating a steady routine to ensure productivity is still achieved.

How?: I'll be going into the specific routine I would recommend implementing when using this approach later in this book as consistency and balance is, I think, essential here to ensure you don't burn out and hit the dreaded **learning slump**.

In terms of the content itself you are learning, I recommend, at the beginning of the 'school year' (which, by the way, can start and end at any given time you desire) sitting down and writing a list of **all of your interests**. For me personally, this comprised of psychology, English literature, philosophy, and criminology. From here, you can research the relevant resources available to you—either free sources available online, or, perhaps, paid courses for your areas of specific interest—and structure a sort of timetable/schedule from there, mixing it up whenever you desire.

Resources: Resources will, of course, vary in terms of what subjects/topics you want to be looking into. However, there are a few sources I have, over the course of my home-schooling, stumbled across and found really useful—all of which covering a range of subjects.

- **Khan Academy** — Already a lifesaver for students worldwide, Khan Academy is a free, non-profit US-based educational organisation founded by Sal Khan (who, by the way, narrates most of the videos and is an absolute legend). Maths, science, IT, and history are, I would say, their 'specialist' subjects and my go-to resource for these in particular. Maths and science lessons are also broken down in terms of age group, so anybody aged from five to 20 can find this platform. Once you create an account, the platform also has a reward system (i.e., a point system and badges) for when you watch videos and complete practice tasks, which is surprisingly motivating. You can also comment on their videos if there is something you want to add or if you need clarification over something, which is great. Overall, Khan is a platform I honestly can't recommend highly enough, and was the backbone of a lot of my schooling routine.

- **John/Hank Green's Crash Courses** — This leads on nicely from Khan Academy, as it was actually through that platform that I found the Greens' Crash Courses. I wouldn't suggest using just these for one given subject, as—as the name suggests—these are short, simple series' discussing the main ideas of a certain topic at hand. Thus, I'd suggest watching these either to a) introduce yourself to the subject so you can get a 'gist' of it, or b) consolidate your knowledge at the end. Nonetheless, these courses are honestly fantastic: they're witty, colourful, engaging, and entertaining, and, from my experience, actually work at drilling in information. They're available on YouTube, and cover a range of subjects (including ecology, biology, AI, history, literature, psychology... and so on), their series' being as short as 10 videos or as long as 50, depending on the breadth of content to cover. They have also fairly recently introduced **Crash Course Kids** for younger watchers.

• **Oxplore** — This is one I more recently discovered and, to people who already use this tool, it may seem strange for me to include it as a suggested learning resource for home-schoolers. However, I would actually say Oxplore is really valuable for a) developing curiosity and critical thinking, b) discovering subjects of interest, and c) increasing general knowledge. Oxplore is essentially a platform founded by Oxford University asking 'big questions' on a daily basis, all of which being, in my opinion, highly thought-provoking and relevant questions to today: past questions have included whether schooling was better in the 1900s, whether there is life after death, and whether time travel would ever be possible—and, as miscellaneous as these may sound, the platform then goes into a critical analysis of these questions, interviewing experts for both sides of the argument and breaking down the history of such a question before quizzing the user on the information provided, ending the session with your final vote on the answer to the question. I would highly recommend getting into the habit of using this platform once a day—either at the beginning or at the end of your working day—, as it requires minimal effort and brain power and yet is, in my opinion, highly valuable, leaving you more able and (hopefully!) confident in engaging in debates and discussions concerning today's state of affairs.

- **Online Academies and NCC Home Learning** — I have grouped both these resources together as the both provide a very similar service: the provision of online courses, with a legitimate qualification at the end—although not in partnership with any of the main UK exam boards. Online Academies especially covers pretty much every subject I can imagine—from psychology and criminology to sports to spiritualty—, and both platforms provide some form of qualification at the end of most of their courses (it was actually through OA that I managed to get a Distinction in a Level 3 Psychology Diploma at age 12—something a lot of adults dream of doing!). Both platforms are great and, in terms of the content they provide, I cannot applaud them enough. Both tend to cost a fair chunk of money (for example, NCC's Criminal Profiling courses altogether currently cost over £400), but I would say these are *highly* worth it in terms of the quality of content you are provided with—plus, they both have a pretty amazing loyalty scheme whereby once you buy one course, you get considerable discounts on a second and third. OA and NCC are also things to look out for on

Groupon and other money-saving websites, as they frequently pop up there, again, with considerable discounts. Something to note before in investing in one of these courses: I would say OA is very much so for **independent, self-driven learners** as there is no deadline for course completion, and the lessons are simply provided in document format, followed by a modular quiz at the end; there is **no in-course support**, and simply relies on your own interest in the subject and ability to revise effectively. On the other hand, NCC provides **online tutors** that you can contact whenever via their emailing system. Your work is also sent and marked by that same tutor, and there is also deadline for completion of your course (usually one year long) after which your tutor support will expire and course content will disappear—ultimately acting as an incentive for completion. I really enjoy both platforms, and I suppose it takes knowing the **kind of learner you are** to know which you would be most suited to. I'm a very independent and self-reliant learner and dislike being forced to complete something by a given time, and so was highly suited to OA—although I also found having a tutor via NCC very helpful and, in some ways, reassuring as I constantly knew I was on the right track. Either way, I recommend looking into both and seeing which (if any) strike your fancy.

• **Duolingo** — You may already be acquainted with Duo the Owl, as Duolingo is currently the most popular language-learning platform out there with an estimated 300,000,000 users. Duolingo is no stranger to criticism by its users, but I have found that, like with anything, this resource can help you make leaps and bounds in terms of learning with effective revision, application, and consistency. Duolingo is a free online platform currently teaching 24 languages (including French, Spanish, Korean, Greek, Russian, Hindi, and Swahili) through mini daily exercises aimed at expanding vocabulary and learning grammar—and, ultimately, enhancing reading, writing, and speaking skills. It implements a daily challenge to encourage users to get their golden 'five minutes a day' and, unknown to some, has a range of features besides its daily mini exercises, such as one where you can talk with users fluent in the language you're learning, be read stories with basic plots to get used to reading and listening in your chosen language, and, more recently, podcasts in the language of interest—all of which encouraging **learning through interaction**, which, as we've established, is pivotal across the board. Considering becoming fluent in a second language is a life goal of many, I would highly recommend taking advantage of your newly found spare time by looking into doing so—and I honestly think Duolingo is a brilliant starting point here. As someone who has used what feels like every free language-learning platform out there (including Busuu, Memrise, and Babbel), I'd say Duolingo comes out on top in terms of its format, order of teaching, and interactive nature.

- **Yousician** — Another platform you may or may not have heard of, Yousician is a free app that teaches—you guessed it—how to play instruments. It was through this that I learnt to play guitar in early 2017, something I'd always wanted to do but for some reason brushed off as something

I'd just never be able to—and the possibilities don't stop there as this app also teaches piano, ukulele, and bass. Like language-learning, learning to play an instrument is a skill I honestly think everyone would be a lot happier having: it's a *major* stress reliever, and the sense of accomplishment after successfully learning to play is honestly immense. Yousician is a fantastic starting point for this: it's easy to understand and begins from the very basics through a combination of videos and exercises, and, similarly to Khan and Duolingo, it also has a reward system, this time in the form of Levels—and, with consistent daily practice, I'd say it's feasible you will be able to play your instrument at a decent level within just a couple of months of using this app.

Advantages: As you may or may not be able to tell, I'm a massive advocate of this home-schooling approach, and found it gave me a lot of fulfilment personally. The main advantage here, of course, is the fact that **you're learning what you want to** without the constraints of a curriculum, (hopefully) in effective manners and **in ways you want to be learning them**. For me, this approach struck the perfect balance between freedom and structure, creativity and productivity. I allowed myself to go off on tangents in my learning, to allow a chain reaction of curiosity when something random on my page piqued curiosity, but would also always have a to-do list at hand to ensure all my overarching learning goals of the day were achieved. This approach, when implemented properly, spurs **independence** and, in my experience, **sparks a love for learning**—and, considering all disciplines intertwine in some way, I have found I have a pretty well-rounded knowledge in certain arenas in biology, history, linguistics, even—simply by studying whatever interested me as and when I came across it.

Disadvantages: The clearest and most frequently occurring disadvantage here, I've found, is when motivation runs low, as motivation is the foundation to this approach. **If you don't want to learn, you're not going to**, and that's all it comes down to. I'll be going into this in more depth later (when we cover my recommended routine for this approach), but this is where it becomes really important for you to be able to identify when you need a break or, perhaps, when you simply need to reshuffle your schedule a little, as the worst thing you can do here is to just **continue with what you're already doing** and realise—after a week, two weeks, a month—that you've **learnt nothing**. Something leading from this that I wouldn't particularly view as a disadvantage myself but a lot of people would is the degree of **self-awareness** required here: you need to stay on top of your game in checking in with yourself frequently. Is the way you're currently teaching yourself this subject reaping the best possible results? Are you working at the time of day you should be? Are you working yourself too hard/not enough? Are you actively engaging in your learning? The reality is that it's **far too easy to get lazy with this method**—you can stick on a video about economics all you want, but that's not your job done—, and so this **self-regulation** is pivotal.

My Recommendations: As touched on above, my main piece of advice is to always keep some form of structure and routine in your studies here—otherwise 'learn what you want' is a little too vague, and thus lends the way to you feeling a little adrift a little later down the line. You still want to be able to track your progress in some way and, as discussed previously, the self-setting and actualising of goals is super important and a very viable skill home-schoolers generally find themselves able to achieve. This is something I very deliberately focus on heavily in my online self-teaching program, as this tangible goal-setting and -completing naturally forms the backbone of this approach's success; even when we're not necessarily following a curriculum, it's essential to have small-scale daily goals you're completing so as to achieve your larger life goals. Another thing I would suggest when implementing this method is to **keep your mind open**: oftentimes we put ourselves in a box without even realising and condition our brains into thinking we'd only be 'good at' a handful of similar subjects—which was very much so the case with me at the beginning of my home-schooling. School seems to have a way of knocking our confidence from a very young age in certain subjects—in my case, maths and science—, and we usually carry these beliefs about ourselves and our skills into home-schooling, when picking our subjects. However, I encourage you to have an open mind and perhaps try and start from scratch with a couple of subjects you never quite warmed to. There is no such thing as being 'naturally better' at English-related or maths-related subjects, nor is there such thing as a 'more right-/left-brained person'; you're just as capable as the next person at physics or Spanish or art. **Get out of your comfort zone** and if you still don't enjoy the subject, at least you know that's because of your own personal preferences, and not an institution's.

So, there you have it: the four main types of home-schooling. There are, of course, more that people choose to use, but hopefully the above can give you some form of a starting point and a gist for what a lot of home-schoolers' daily lives entail. Home-schooling is rarely as linear as simply shifting the classroom experience to the home-schooler's bedroom, as we can hopefully appreciate at this point, and, by the end of their experiences, most home-schoolers have formulated their own completely unique strategy tailored to them completely.

Don't be afraid to use some trial-and-error during the early stages of home-schooling; being honest, it's highly unlikely you're going to uptake the perfect approach from the get-go. It can take a while to actually figure out how you learn best and what structure fits with you the best, and that's okay—**you've got time**, and time spent figuring yourself out isn't time wasted: it's actually a part of the learning experience. Saying this, with some guidance from this book as a starting point, you will hopefully be able to shave off some of this time and pinpoint the approach and learning style you feel is right for you.

As a starting point, I suggest selecting the method above that you feel most drawn to, and perhaps try it out for a week or so. If you like the sound of more than one, then feel free to combine them, as most people do—and if you like the sound of none, you can either research some alternative methods, or simply dive straight into what feels right. Trust your intuition and don't worry about getting it perfect right away: all will ultimately fall into place.

EXAMS AND FINANCES:
WHAT YOU NEED TO KNOW

E XAMS: WHAT IT FEELS the entirety of our educations lead up to, every single moment of learning, work, revision, and extra research coming down to those couple of hours in an exam hall. In school, we have qualified teachers spoon-feeding us the information we need to pass, providing us with extra work and guiding us through the bumps in the road and the moments of panic. Little to our knowledge at the time, there are also a variety of other processes going on behind the scenes in order to ensure exams run smoothly: exam boards are decided upon years before the date, the necessary paperwork is signed, and the exam halls are booked.

These processes are perhaps things you have never thought about before—or at least, not until you began considering home-schooling—, and it is in this section that I will be clearing up any of the confusion you may have around exams as a private candidate (i.e., what you will/would be as a home-schooler). I'll also be covering the legalities behind education and examinations (i.e., whether you have to take them in the first place), as well as how you can actually go about sitting exams (in terms of the things you'll physically have to do and look into to sit an exam), and, of course, my own recommendations for everything about exams.

Legalities: Are You Legally Obligated to Sit Exams?

There is a lot about the school system that we just don't seem to question and simply go along with—and, for the most part, I feel this is very much so the case with exams. Children and adults alike (myself included, before I became home-schooled) seem to take it as a given that exams are just something we **have to do**. For me personally, I actually never thought about this through a legal lens: I just assumed that in order to access good education and, later, an optimal career, you had to take all exams that come your way and do well in them, and that was it.

So, let's just cut to the chase: no, it is not illegal to be home-schooled or to not sit any exams—nor does doing so make you completely unemployable. What *is* illegal is to not provide your child with a **sufficient education** (or, as per www.gov.uk: You must make sure your child receives a full-time education from the age of five). This may sound difficult to believe considering the extent to which most of our brains have been conditioned into believing exams and their results are the be all and end all of our lives, but I can assure you that if you—say, an aspiring astrophysicist—decide not to sit an English Literature GCSE at age 16, your future employer won't regard you any differently as they will someone with that qualification.

However, what *will* jeopardise such goals, particularly in cases such as the above, is a lack of forward-thinking—which leads us on nicely to our second section.

What Exams Should You Sit?

So, we've established that you don't *have* to sit any exams whatsoever—but does that mean there aren't any you *should* sit?

My simple answer to this would be no. To demonstrate this, let's go back to our example from above—i.e., that of somebody who wants to be an astrophysicist. Clearly, you wouldn't need that English Literature GCSE in order to progress onto such a career. However, it should be fairly intuitive that a Maths GCSE and a Physics GCSE certainly wouldn't go amiss here—and that continuing those subjects into A-Level would be a must.

Similarly, say you want to study linguistics at university: suddenly that Literature GCSE would be very valuable! Thus, if you already have an idea of what you want to be doing in the future, it is essential you look into this in terms of the qualifications, work experience, etc. that would be required for you to secure a place in such a field. For those living in the UK, I would strongly suggest using the UCAS website as a point of reference here, as they list the qualifications and skillsets required for a given field.

In terms of GCSEs, I would personally say **everyone** should sit an English Language GCSE and a Maths GCSE, for two reasons: a) the fact that these are core subjects that do, ultimately, ensure you are sufficiently literate and numerate, and b) life simply being made a whole lot easier in terms of applications (whether that be college, university, apprenticeships, or jobs), as these are the only two GCSEs almost all esteemed educating bodies and employers seem to want you to have.

You may choose to sit more, and that's completely fine—it certainly can't hurt! However, I would personally say other GCSEs **aren't a necessity**, and that you can get other qualifications with the same money (we'll go into the finances behind GCSEs in a moment) that are actually of a **higher level** and will thus be viewed with **higher regard**—and will, more to the point, equip you better for the future.

For example: The career path I originally planned for was criminal psychology, and so it seemed more important to invest my time and money into criminology, psychology, and criminal psychology courses and qualifications, rather than studying for a Psychology GCSE—and it is with these qualifications that I got into the best college in my area with an unconditional offer. Doing something different to everybody else may feel a little risky, but I've found this actually gives you an edge above other candidates: it shows independence and an ability to think outside the box.

Not sure on what you want to do in the future? It's here that I would give you the same advice as most teachers, parents, and fellow/ex-students that have their heads screwed on will: **pursue what interests you**. I personally would also suggest seeking some qualifications in these sectors (as in, post-GCSE qualifications) just so these are something to fall back on.

In summary: I would highly advise still sitting English Language and Maths GCSEs considering these subjects are an integral part of **any** course or job, and my recommendations in terms of post-GCSE qualifications (e.g., A-Levels; BTECs; NVQs, etc.) differ on a case-by-case basis: some careers don't necessarily require any qualifications whatsoever (e.g., sales and marketing; military security; chauffeuring), whilst others absolutely require qualifications showcasing your skills in that area (e.g., lawyers; surgeons). As mentioned above, it's always a good idea to **look into your options** and establish what is required of you, qualifications-wise, within a certain career path—as is allowing yourself to have something to fall back on if not all goes to plan.

Basically, it's a good idea to have some qualifications, but you can be flexible in how you do so: it may be that you decide to do two A-Levels whilst you complete work experience—or that an apprenticeship is the way to go for you. Either way, just make sure you properly weigh up your options and, if possible, have some sort of game-plan going forward.

How Do You Sit Exams?

This section is, as you may expect, a pretty big and important bit—and encloses information I 100% wish I'd have known from the onset of my home-schooling experience so that I could have made some more informed decisions about exams in advance. This is the *how* to exams within home-schooling.

Note: This section does not cover how to *study* for exams, but is purely the steps you need to take in order to actually **apply** for and **sit** exams as a private candidate (although, notably, how to teach yourself in such a way that you can easily recall this information later on down the line is the focal point of my teachings in my online program, The Learning Success Academy).

One final point of note before we begin: **you can sit any exams at any age**. Thus, you don't have to wait until the May/June following Year 11 to sit your GCSEs—nor do you have to sit all your GCSEs in one go. However, you do have to adhere to the dates at which the exams are ongoing (usually in either in May/June or November)—in other words, you can't just randomly decide to sit an exam on any given day of any given month. The dates at which exams are ongoing are predetermined and decided by the exam board at hand, and can be found on their website.

A quick disclaimer before we begin: the below information all concerns exams **within the UK**. I have no expertise whatsoever in terms of how you would go about sitting exams anywhere else, and so any information below regarding selecting exam boards and applying for and sitting exams is **all** wholly based on the UK examination system.

Let's begin.

Exam Boards

Exam boards are (in the UK) the people responsible for the outlining and awarding of qualifications, and are all governed by the Office of the Regulators of Qualifications (more commonly referred to as Ofqual). Most schools will use different exam boards for different subjects, and it is important to remember that **different exam boards have different curricula**—i.e., the stuff they want you to learn that will be in the exam. This is why it is so important to buy resources approved by your exam board, as content within such resources will vary.

The main exam boards in the UK are:
- Assessment and Qualifications Alliance (AQA)
- Edexcel
- Oxford, Cambridge and RSA Examinations (OCR)
- Welsh Joint Education Committee (WJEC)
- Council for the Curriculum, Examinations & Assessment (CCEA).

Thus, selecting your exam board(s) is your first step in terms of your exams, as this should occur **before** you start studying for such subjects (for the reason cited above).

Notably, WJEC is the Welsh exam board and CCEA the Northern Irish one. Some schools outside of Wales (but still in the UK) have started implementing its syllabus for some subjects (although this is less common), whereas CCEA is reserved exclusively, as of 2012, for students in Northern Ireland only.

All of these exam boards are very similar: all subject content is determined by the Department for Education—including what is taught and how it is assessed within exams—, and so there isn't much room for variation in terms of what is taught and how it is assessed. This is, of course, very important so that all students across the UK are assessed equally.

However, as may be expected, there are *slight* variations in terms of this content—particularly in terms of the general format of test papers, as well as the weightings of AOs (Assessment Objectives) within exams and how much influence Non-Exam Assessments (NEAs)—i.e., coursework—, if there is any, have on a final grade. All exams are, however, marked fairly, all examiners (the people employed by the exam boards who mark the papers) having to adhere to the scheme of assessment exactly. Thus, a 6 in GCSE Maths with OCR is not going to differ much from a 6 in GCSE Maths with Edexcel.

This contradicts a lot of people's misconceptions regarding exam boards, as there is this overall idea that some exam boards are 'easier' than others. Whilst I'd like to be able to say this belief derives from the annual reports exam boards release concerning the grades achieved by their students, I do believe it is actually word of mouth that is the real culprit here. When I joined public education again at the onset of Year 12 (before reverting back to home-education two months later—a testament to home-schooling in itself!), the air was charged with debates about exam boards: Molly was predicted a 9 in History but only got a 6, whereas Jake was predicted to fail but passed with flying colours. Considering Molly was with AQA and Jake with OCR, it *must* have just been AQA trying to 'screw her over'—when in reality, the scheme of assessment and grade boundaries for those exam boards were so close, it seems far likelier that the simpler and less conspiracy-centred option is true: Jake just performed better in the exam.

Indeed, I think it is fair to say that the vast majority—if not *all*—of the opinions on exam boards we hear—both positive and negative—originate from the students themselves. This is, of course, an unreliable source—not only because emotions tend to run high here, but also because no one student will sit an exam for one given subject with more than one exam board. Thus, nobody is really in a position to compare two exam boards for a given subject anyway, no matter how objective they remain.

What I'm trying to get at here is that **no exam board is 'easier' or more lenient than the others**. There's no way to cheat the system by going for an easier exam board, nor is there any chance that you will end up with a lower grade in a given subject because you sat it with one exam board rather than another. There will always be differences in performance across exam boards each year, but this is more often than not a reflection on the **students** who just so happen to be sitting with a given exam board, not the exam board itself.

So, if all of these exam boards are so similar, how can you go about selecting which one(s) to use for each subject?

When it comes to GCSEs, if the student in question has already attended public school in either Key Stage 3 (i.e., between Year 7 and Year 9) or Key Stage 4 (between Year 10 and Year 11)—i.e., during secondary school—, then the easiest and most intuitive thing to do would be to simply continue learning with the exam board(s) they were whilst in school; that way, they can simply pick up where they left off in school and carry on with the curriculum as they were. This also means any resources they were given by the school will still be useful, and, for older learners (Key Stage 4), will also most likely mean they will already be familiar with the scheme of assessment, exam paper layouts, etc.

The same logic applies for A-Level students: if the student left public schooling whilst in Year 12/13—i.e., whilst studying for their exams—, it makes far more sense to just continue with the exam board(s) they were learning with before than selecting a new one. For example, all my A-Level subjects in Year 12 were with AQA, and so that is the exam board I began studying all my A-Levels in accordance with at home.

If, however, the student has not yet begun the curriculum for the exams in question, then it is completely up to you to select the exam board you desire. Personally, I recommend briefly going through each exam board's specification (subject content), layout of test papers, etc. and see if any in particular appeal to you more than others: remember, each exam board varies *slightly* in terms of approach, so it seems probably one would pull you in more.

If, however, this is not the case, my advice would simply be to go for the most popular exam board for your subject at hand. If you live in Wales, this will always be WJEC; if you live in Northern Ireland, this will always be CCEA; and if you live in England or Scotland, this is usually AQA for essay-based subjects (i.e., English Language; English Literature; History; Politics; Religious Education, etc.) and Edexcel for more maths-/science-based subjects. OCR, meanwhile, seems to be implemented slightly less frequently—but by no means rarely—for each subject.

My reason for recommending the exam board that is most popular is, again, not because this means they are 'better', but because this usually means there are more resources available—not necessarily in terms of official resources from the exam board itself (textbooks, past papers, etc.), but in terms of more miscellaneous resources—most of which being online (YouTube personalities such as Mr Bruff and Mr Salles being fantastic for GCSE AQA English, for example)—and the more help available, the better.

Notably, if you choose to study for exams with the aid of online courses (which we'll explore shortly), more often than not these courses will have already been created in mind of a specific exam board's curriculum—so **you won't have to choose for yourself after all**.

Once you have selected your exam board(s), there is now nothing more you need to do except begin studying for those exams in accordance with the respective curriculum—you don't have to go through any official 'signing up' process or anything of the sort to start studying for their curriculum. The only official application process you have to undergo is when it comes to actually applying to sit the exams, which you don't have to do until five months or so before you plan on sitting them—which, of course, we will also be going through shortly.

IGCSEs

A very popular alternative to traditional GCSE exams amongst distance learners, international students, and many top UK independent schools (Eton, Harrow, etc.) is IGCSEs (International GCSEs). These were initially introduced in 1988, and are generally agreed to be more similar to O-Levels (i.e., the equivalent of GCSEs between 1951-1988) than current GCSEs. IGCSEs are essentially the same as GCSEs in terms of how they are regarded by schools, employers, etc., but differ in terms of:

- **The curriculum.** Although very similar to that of GCSEs, IGCSE curricula are generally regarded as more challenging for students. This curriculum is also better adapted in mind of distance learners, as they were originally put forward to create an even playing field for everybody—in other words, lessons tend to be 'broken down' a lot more.

- **Applying for exams.** Perhaps why this is such a popular option amongst distance learners is the fact that there are far less administrative steps you have to go through in order to apply for exams (a process we will go through in a moment).
- **NEAs.** Similar to the above reason (as it tends to make the exam application far easier for distance learners), IGCSE courses usually require little to no coursework (again, something else we'll delve into in the next section).

Notably, it's also the following exam boards that supply such qualifications in the UK:

- Edexcel
- AQA
- Cambridge Assessment International Education (ICE).

So, what are better: GCSEs or IGCSEs?

The jury is out with this one, and I personally cannot give my own personal opinion on this matter as I have no experience with IGCSEs (I only didn't choose to sit them because I didn't know they even existed when the time came!), but what I can say is that out of the other home-schooled people I have known, it's been about 50-50 whether they have done traditional GCSEs or IGCSEs—and the reviews seem to be pretty similar for both.

Thus, there is no definitive answer—just what works for you (as is becoming a recurring theme throughout this book!). Have a look into both and see which course suits you most, and go from there.

Distance Learning Programmes (DLPs)

When home-schoolers choose to follow the National Curriculum and sit public exams, a very popular route is to sign up for Distance Learning Programs (DLPs), created specifically in mind of meeting the specification of a specific exam board.

It is easy to understand why this is a very popular route: as mentioned above, your exam board is oftentimes selected for you, all lessons are created for you at your disposal, the platform will usually book all of your exams for you—which can be a massive stress relief at the time—, and, more often than not, you will be assigned online tutors who you can contact anytime. In other words, this method to learning a curriculum is a rather convenient, straightforward, and safe one, as there is never the risk of you missing out any content you need to know—so long as you complete all the units in time!

What I will say about DLPs is that many users struggle when it comes to both short- and long-term time-management in this respect, either a) creating an **unrealistic** study plan upon their starting the course, or b) not creating a study plan at all, letting months (and sometimes even years!) go by before realising, too late, that they physically do not have enough time let to cover all the content before exam season. Both situations are *extremely* stressful, as an understatement, and are very easy mistakes to make considering there is nobody there except you to hold you accountable for your progress. (Any online tutors you may be assigned are under no obligation to ensure you are staying on-track, deadline-wise.) It is because of this that I would highly advise that you check out my Top 3 Rookie Mistakes Home-Schoolers Make When Scheduling booklet before investing in some DLPs, which is free for download at:

https://www.fayepaige.co/readersfreebie

Notably, falling behind is super easy to do when you are not equipped with the right knowledge, and this is something you certainly do not want to be doing when you are using DLPs! This guide details every basic mistake I have made personally when using DLPs and when using the Individual Courses method (detailed in our What Are The Different Routes Of Home-Schooling? section) so that you can avoid falling down that slippery slope of ineffective scheduling from the get-go and so you are ready to ace your exams once exam season rolls around.

There are a wealth of platforms that offer these courses, the most popular ones being **ICS Learn**—for GCSEs, A-Levels, and IGCSEs (but more on IGCSEs later)—, the **National**

Extension College (NEC)—for GCSEs and A-Levels—, **CloudLearn**—again, for GCSEs and A-Levels—, **Oxford Opening Learning**—for GCSEs, IGCSEs, and A-Levels—, and, of course, the **Open University (OU)**—for degrees and certificates.

The only platform from the above that I have personal experience with and thus feel able to give my complete opinion on is NEC, as this is the platform I (as I am writing this) used to study for my A-Levels; however, it seems the vast majority of Distance Learning Platforms that provide courses in mind of specific examinations (i.e., GCSEs; A-Levels; degrees) offer a very similar service and general format. These are:

- Text-based modules: These are your lessons, which are usually available either within their website, or in physical paper form (which they typically deliver to you).
- One-to-one tutor support: You will typically be assigned a tutor per subject once you have enrolled in a course, who you can contact within the platform for support concerning your courses whenever you need.
- The setting and marking of assignments: Of course, if you are going to sit external examinations, it is highly important that you assess yourself in some way on a regular basis to ensure you are on the right track—and, thus, assignments are always assigned—usually, in my experience, at the end of each unit—to ensure

understanding and track progress, and are typically marked by your tutor.

- In-website chatrooms: Chatrooms for the students enrolled on such platforms are also a common occurrence here, and these have, in my experience, proven to be more helpful than you may expect. Whether you have specific questions about a certain part of your course, you are seeking advice, or you simply want to strike up conversation and build connections with fellow distance learners, chatrooms can make the overall distance learning process far more enjoyable.

As touched on in the previous section, if you choose to enrol with platforms such as the above, your exam board(s) will almost always be selected for you. Indeed, whenever you sign up for such courses, you will usually receive some form of 'Welcome Pack' detailing everything you need to know about enrolling for and studying for exams—including the specification your course has been made for. If you don't receive such a pack, this information will always be available on the platform's website.

For example, it is clearly displayed on the Dashboard of my NEC Profile that my A-Level English Literature course is preparing me for the A-Level Specification 7712 exams—i.e., AQA AS and A-Level English Literature A. Thus, whenever I want, say, past papers for revision, or to look into the specification in more depth, I know that this is the spec I should be going off.

Now, for the most relevant question: should you buy these DLPs if you are, indeed, planning on sitting external examinations?

There is not one correct answer to this question, as it all comes down to how *you* feel you would learn best, bearing in mind both how you learn best and the nature of the subject matter itself; however, what I will say is that whether you decide to use such platforms or not, when it comes to studying for external exams, some form of structure is an absolute necessity. This is non-negotiable: drift aimlessly through a specification at any pace you want and you run the risk of not only not completing the subject matter in time, but also in not understanding the content thoroughly and thus giving yourself a fighting chance of actually doing well in exams. (Again, make sure you download my Top 3 Rookie Mistakes Home-Schoolers Make When Scheduling if you plan on using DLPs so this doesn't happen to you.)

So, what do I actually recommend here? Are online courses always the best route to take when it comes to studying for exams, or can alternative methods work just as well?

My personal advise would be that, when it comes to **GCSE exams** specifically, DLPs aren't always necessary; they certainly can't do any harm, but considering they are not cheap by any means for many (I'll go into the finances of online courses later) and most people end up taking between eight and 12 GCSE subjects altogether, I would say they are by no means necessary. If I had taken this many GCSEs (which was what I originally planned to do before learning more about the financial implications of doing so), I believe I would have likely only bought courses for a select few subjects I either really struggled with, or needed that extra reassurance with. Otherwise, I do believe that with the right routine, structure, and forward-thinking, any GCSE curriculum can be learnt efficiently through other, more readily available sources.

What about learning an **IGCSE curriculum**? Does *this* approach require you to use official Distance Learning Platforms specifically for the IGCSE curricula? My advice here (again, purely going off what I've heard from other people's experiences—I don't have my own experience to go off) would be similar to that of GCSEs: I certainly wouldn't say it is necessary, as all exam boards' specifications are available on their websites, and textbooks specific to those specifications are widely available. However, I've found that home-schoolers typically tend to lean more towards buying courses for these curricula—not because this is necessary, but because IGCSEs are, for most, quite an **unfamiliar** concept, so they feel more reassured by purchasing such courses (as the content, as mentioned above, does vary in terms of what is taught, how it is taught, and how it is assessed within the exams). Thus, if you would feel uneasy going for such curricula due to this foreignness, I'd suggest you doing the same.

On the contrary, when it comes to **A-Level exams**, whereby the content and, in turn, the exams are designed to be far denser and more challenging than that of a given GCSE subject, I do feel it is somewhat necessary to seek further assistance than that provided by the Internet, textbooks, etc., and that the courses offered by DLPs are, in this respect, designed not just to teach you the curriculum at hand, but also to prepare you for the exams themselves—including the kind of format you are expected to write according to AOs, how to revise for them, external resources you should be looking into to further your learning, etc. As much as these things are also somewhat relevant for GCSE exams, A-Levels inherently tend to go a lot further with this, not just testing for knowledge or the application of knowledge in the same way GCSEs do, but also for a sort of flare, skill, and intuition in applying the content at hand. Thus, I would highly recommend seeking online courses to aid you in studying for A-Level exams, but (as I keep stressing!) with the aforementioned knowledge that a **high degree of discipline, forward-thinking**, and **ability to schedule and manage your time** will be absolutely necessary here. I'm not saying this to stress you out or make out that DLPs are super difficult to use (they're not), but just so I can be certain that I've set you off on the right foot if this is a route you choose to pursue.

If you do indeed choose to seek the assistance of online courses to accompany you during your studying for external exams, then I recommend researching a variety of different DLPs—and there are many, not just the ones mentioned in this section!—that offer such courses and seeing which one appeals to you the most—whether that's in terms of the services they provide, their prices, or the general layout of their platform.

Applying for Exams

Now we have cleared up everything you need to know in regard to setting yourself up for *studying* for exams, let us delve into the specifics of how to actually enrol for and *sit* those exams.

As mentioned above, if you are signed up to Distance Learning Platforms, more often than not, these platforms will arrange all of your examinations for you, so if you are currently using/planning on using such platforms, don't worry about this section—they'll contact you regarding any details to do with your examinations closer to the time.

If, however, this isn't the case for you and you're applying for exams completely from scratch, you'll need to complete the following step-by-step process in order to sit your exams.

- **Find an exam centre near you.** An exam centre is basically a place that is approved by your exam board(s) for you to sit your exam(s). This exam centre is where other people will also be sitting the same exam as you, and more often than not your nearest exam centre will be a school or college. Thus, your first task is to essentially call around at all your local schools and see if they accept **private candidates** (which is what you are!)—i.e., see if they'd be happy for you to sit your exam(s) there. This is something you want to start doing relatively early—preferably **at least**

four months before your exam. This is because a) your exam board will always have an application deadline that is around this time (which you can find on the exam board's website and you **must** be aware of and adhere to); b) **this process can take a while**, as a lot of places either don't accept private candidates at all, or have very limited availability for such applicants; and c) when you *do* find a suitable exam centre, they will need time to register you for your exam(s).

Tip: Some exam board websites will actually have a list of places that accept private candidates according to area (e.g., Edexcel); however, **don't stop at these lists**, as these are only centres they have specifically asked the exam board to put on their website. If there isn't one particularly close to you on there, contact some of the schools that are close to you first, and you might strike lucky.

- **Supply that exam centre with your details.** As mentioned above, it is your selected exam centre that will be completing the application process for your exam(s) for you, so they will need your details so the qualification is completely yours in the end. Typically, they will require the following information:
  - **Your full name**
  - **Your address**
  - **Your postcode**
  - **Your date of birth**

- **Your phone number**
- **Whether you have any coursework to submit**
- **The subject's/subjects' details (title, exam code, etc.)**
- **Your Unique Candidate Identifier (UCI).** This is just the number code you will have been assigned if you've sat any exams in the past. If you haven't, don't worry about it: you'll be given one during the registration process. If you have, you'll be able to find it on any results sheets you've received in the past. Can't find it? Don't worry; just contact the exam centre you sat the exam(s) with at the time, and they'll have all the information for you.
- **Your bank details.**
- **Await further instruction.** Once the application process is complete, you will likely hear from your exam centre again a couple of weeks or so before the exam is due to take place with any further details you may need before going into the exam. This can include the room number you'll be sitting the exam in, time the exam is due to begin, any details you will need to bring with you as proof of identity, etc.

And that's that! As mentioned in the first bullet point, this process of finding an appropriate exam centre, sending through and processing all your details, and actually registering for your exam(s) can be a fairly lengthy process, so my main advice here would be to **give yourself plenty of**

time before the application deadline. This way, you'll be able to take all the time you need to actually look into all the exam centres near you, contact them all, allow time for them to respond, and select the one that is best for you. A home-schooler's worst nightmare is to leave this whole process too late and for none of the exam centres near them to have any availability for private candidates left, so leave plenty of time to ensure you can secure your place in that exam hall.

What about IGCSEs? I mentioned in the previous section that one of the main reasons for IGCSEs being a popular option amongst distance learners is the fact that there tend to be less administrative steps to applying for these exams—and, whilst this is true, as it certainly is considered to be much easier to apply for IGCSE exams than GCSE exams as a private candidate once you have found an exam centre that will take you on, actually getting to that stage—finding an appropriate exam centre—is typically a more difficult process than when you're looking to sit GCSE exams. This won't be the case for everyone sitting IGCSEs, but if it's mainly state-owned secondary schools and colleges you're looking at, these institutes are likely going to be unfamiliar with IGCSE exams, and are thus typically wearier to take on such private candidates.

Because of this, I'd suggest mainly calling around at private tuition centres, private schools, and independent schools—i.e., places that are more likely to already be familiar with IGCSEs—if you are struggling to find somewhere.

In terms of the actual exam application process, you'll have to follow the same process as in the process for GCSEs: find an exam centre that is happy to take you on (and leave yourself plenty of time to do so!), supply them with any details they need (likely far less than will be needed for GCSE application), and await further instruction.

NEAs

Non-Exam Assessments (NEAs) are—you guessed it!—assessments that take place outside of the exam setting that some subjects require in order for you to be able to gain your full qualification. These are practical in nature, and more often than not, this is coursework that will contribute to your overall grade in a specific subject—usually the likes of art, D&T, English, etc., as well as some science-related subjects, as these often require you to do practical assessments, and language subjects (e.g., French; German) for speaking assessments. Less frequently—such as in GCSE English Language—, this is an assessment that actually won't contribute to your final grade, but is still necessary for you to do, as per your exam board.

For example, a big chunk of your grade in A-Level Art will often be coursework (depending on the exam board, perhaps one big art piece, or a themed sketchbook). On the other hand, for GCSE English Language, your NEA will often be some kind of talk dedicated to a topic of your choosing. This latter example will be filmed, sent to your exam board, and graded separately to your actual English Language GCSE grade.

So, if coursework is a part of your subject's specification, how does this work in the context of home-schooling?

Again, if you are completing your course through a Distance Learning Program, they will usually submit all your coursework for you, so don't worry about this section if this is the case for you.

As you may expect, your exam centre comes into this section again. If this is a practical assessment (e.g., speaking; a scientific practical; a theatrical performance, etc.), it will wholly be your exam centre's responsibility to:

- **Supervise you** whilst conducting this assessment (e.g., oversee a scientific practical);
- **Authenticate the work**;
- Meet the exam board's **requirements** for the assessment;
- **Assess** the work;
- **Apply you** for the assessment;
- **Accommodate you** for the assessment.

All of the above besides the first point (i.e., supervision) and the last (i.e., accommodate you) will also be required for material assessments (e.g., artwork; essays; research papers), as a higher body will not need to oversee this process but will still have to ensure the NEA meets the exam board's requirements.

As mentioned above, it is while you're sending your details for your exams to your exam board that you will also need to mention whether you have any NEAs that will also need to be sent to the exam board. Once you have done so, if you need to complete any **practical** assessments, your exam centre will likely call you in a couple of months before your exam so you can complete your assessment. When it comes to **material** assessments, on the other hand, they'll usually send you a date after the registration process for when they'll need you to send the document/piece over for submission.

As in the case of the examinations themselves, exam boards also have deadlines for NEA submissions, which are available on their websites—and, again, as is the case for examinations, your exam centre will likely have their own earlier deadline for when they want to have made these applications, so make sure you know where you stand in terms of timing. Usually, the exam board's deadline for NEA submission is between **six weeks and two months before the actual exam is due to take place**, whilst the exam centre deadlines tend to be a lot earlier—usually a couple of months before the exam board's deadline. Thus, as is the case for examinations, I would recommend leaving yourself **plenty of time** before these deadlines so you can definitely get everything sorted in time.

Exam Results

So, you've studied, booked, and sat your exams; now where do results come in?

Your results for any examinations—whether that be GCSEs, IGCSEs, or A-Levels—will be released at the same time as everybody else's. For summer exam series' (i.e., those occurring between May-June), results will typically be released in mid- to late-August; for November series', on the other hand, results are usually released in mid- to late-January.

In terms of how you will actually receive your exam results, some exam centres will have you come in and collect your results sheet with the rest of their students. However, I've found that it's more often that private candidates will just get emailed their results on the day.

The Finances of Exams — How Much Do They Cost?

And now for the question that seems to haunt all parents once the question of home-schooling arises: how much is all of this actually going to cost?

Before we delve into this matter, please note that the reason I am only discussing finances in terms of exams as a private candidate and not for other home-schooling methods (e.g., the finances of implementing the Charlotte Mason approach) is because these other approaches vary far too much for me to even begin to try to categorise. Any monetary approximation I could give you in terms of any such approaches would automatically be invalid for the vast majority of readers, as the way in which such methods are implemented will vary with pretty much every single home-schooler out there.

The finances involved in preparing, applying, and sitting for exams, however, can be quantified somewhat, and that's what I'm going to be going into in this section.

Again, please bear in mind that **these are just approximations**, and will vary in accordance with what the qualification is, how many exams you are sitting, your selected exam centre, when you're sitting your exams... The list goes on. However, the following breakdown should be fairly accurate in the kind of finances you can expect when sitting exams as a private candidate.

How Much Are Distance Learning Platforms (DLPs)?
Let's start from the beginning of the whole exam process: actually studying for those exams. As explored above, the use of Distance Learning Platforms (DLPs) is the most common route taken by home-schoolers when studying for external exams—mainly for the security this provides, as it automatically gives you a structured path through a given

subject's curriculum, leaving little to no room for error in terms of the content you are learning.

As you may expect, prices vary between DLPs, types of qualification, etc. However, for **GCSE and IGCSE subjects**, these are the average DLP prices for courses for the most common subjects:

- **Maths** — £287.50
- **English Language** — £318.00
- **English Literature** — £349.00
- **Biology** — £285.00
- **Chemistry** — £354.00
- **Religious Studies** — £317.25
- **Geography** — £374.00
- **History** — £311.00

Meanwhile, in terms of **A—Levels**:

- **Maths** – £434.00
- **Biology** – £407.00
- **Psychology** – £374.00
- **Chemistry** – £498.00
- **English Literature** – £406.00
- **Physics** – £486.00
- **Sociology** – £386.00
- **Geography** — £424.00

Now, I don't think many people *wouldn't* look at these numbers and panic a little bit—but please don't worry: all DLPs are aware of the fact that not everybody is able to pay off such a big chunk of money just like that, so all allow for payments in instalments—such instalments usually being between **£15.00-£30.00 per subject per month** over a two-year period, or thereabouts. Thus, if you were to do so with three A-Level subjects, for example, you'd be paying around £68.00 per month for three DLPs—or, alternatively, around £1,280 all in one go, if that's the route you choose.

Remember, home-schooling is something to **break you away from worry** and **give you more flexibility** in your life, so if a less conventional approach to taking exams—such as focusing a year at a time on one A-Level course through your chosen DLP for three years—would suit you better financially, go for it! You're completely in a position to do so.

Going back to my advice concerning these courses in the previous section, whilst I do think they are particularly invaluable when it comes to preparing for A-Levels specifically, I definitely wouldn't say they are necessary for every GCSE subject you sit. Again, everyone will vary with this, but I'd personally say it's best to only buy courses for GCSE subjects you feel you'd need some extra guidance in. However, the choice is entirely yours: some are in a position to buy courses for all their subjects and decide that this is the approach for them, and others decide not to. It is entirely your choice when bearing in mind your circumstances—both financially and academically.

How Much to Apply for Exams?

So, you've studied for your exams, and you're now looking at following the steps listed in our previous section on how to actually apply for those exams. How much are we expecting this to come to? Again, **please bear in mind these costs are approximations**, and that the below estimated prices are just there to give you a gist of the kind of figures you'll be dealing with.

Exam Board Fees

Exam boards have their own fees per qualification that private candidates are to pay for during the process of booking their exams through their chosen exam centre. These are the fees that are usually covered by schools when they are registering their students for such exams.

All of the below approximations are for the total qualification, not just one exam within that qualification.

For the most popular **GCSE and IGCSE exams**, these are the approximate prices you will be looking at to actually book and sit those exams:

- **Maths** – £40.00
- **English Language** – £41.00
- **English Literature** – £40.00
- **Biology** – £40.00
- **Chemistry** – £40.00

- **Religious Studies** – £38.00
- **Geography** – £41.00
- **History** — £41.00

And for the most popular **A—Level exams**:

- **Maths** – £117.00
- **Biology** – £97.00
- **Psychology** – £95.00
- **Chemistry** – £97.00
- **English Literature** – £91.00
- **Physics** – £97.00
- **Sociology** – £93.00
- **Geography** — £111.00

You will typically pay such fees during the application process for your exams via your exam centre (hence why they'll usually ask for your bank details during the application process).

The above charges are the only ones you should expect whilst applying for exams—unless your exam centres add an **additional administration/accommodation charge**, which is common amongst exam centres. This charge covers any administration costs falling on the exam centre's shoulders as a result of managing your entry, sorting any relevant paperwork, paying invigilators, using their facilities, etc., and the amount varies across exam centres; it's at each exam centre's discretion what charge they decide to apply, if any. Whilst some will let you sit for free, others' costs will range from **£15.00-£70.00 per exam** (*not* per qualification; e.g., if you have three Mathematics papers to sit within your Maths GCSE and the exam centre has an admin charge of £30.00, the total here would be £90.00). Considering how much these prices vary, a lot of private candidates spend some time 'shopping around' at local exam centres before settling on the cheapest and/or most convenient one.

Notably, generally speaking, exam centres that are already submitting their students for the **same exams** are far likelier to be a little less demanding in terms of the fee they apply—and, accordingly, those who *aren't* will likely slap on a much larger fee. So, say you're sitting a Geography GCSE exam, it is far likelier that a local secondary school will already be applying their students for those same exams—whilst for a local college, it's considerably less likely that its students would be sitting this exam. Thus, a local secondary school should probably be at the top of your priority list here.

So, taking into account all of the above, a private candidate studying for, say, five GCSE subjects, would be looking at roughly the following total costs **with the relevant DLPs**:

- £1,620.00 for the relevant DLPs (assuming payment is given upfront, rather than with monthly instalments);
- £240.00 for exam application fees;
- And £275.00 for exam centre administration charges (if applicable).

The above hypothetical situation would add up to a grand total of about £2,135.00 by the end of the entire process—or, alternatively, **without the DLPs**, £515.00.

Again, please bear in mind these are purely **approximations** at the time of my writing this book. However, hopefully the above gives you some indication of the kind of fees you will likely be looking at if/when sitting exams as a private candidate.

How Does This Compare to Mainstream Schooling?

Now, I am very aware of the fact that figures such as the above are probably far from reassuring to the average parent/young adult looking into taking exams as/on behalf of a private candidate—and, admittedly (as briefly discussed in our **FAQs** section), home-school is really the financial opposite of mainstream schooling in the sense that, whilst home-school requires larger sums of money at once (which, in the long-term, total to less than what mainstream school would cost), schools tend to spread these costs across a number of years, asking for a £5 donation here and the odd £150 (or more) school trip there.

Whilst mainstream schooling's method of drip-feeding monetary requests will likely easier for the average family to provide, this does not change the fact that, in most cases, your bank balance would actually be worse for wear in mainstream school than home-school.

To bring this point into context, let us break down the total approximate costs I know my mum would have been paying if I had stayed in school during my adolescence. Since we gave an approximate figure above for sitting GCSE exams whilst being home-schooled (and these exams would likely be your only real financial demand while home-schooling during secondary school), let's stick with the theme and approximate the total costs of secondary school.

Again, please bear in mind these are entirely approximations based on my *own* experience during my seven months in a public comprehensive secondary school in the North-West of England. These are not official figures by any means and are here just to give you a rough idea of the average costs of simply participating in school.

- **School Uniform (a new one with the start of each school year):** £133.50/year (Total across five years: **£667.50**)
- **School Lunches:** £20/week (Total across five years: **£3,900**)
- **School Trips:** £200/trip (Total across five years: **£400**)
- **Charity events:** £5/event (Total across five years: **£150**)
- **Travel:** £2.50/day (Child's day bus ticket) (Total across five years: **£2,437.50**)
- **Stationery, bags, etc.:** £150/year (Total across five years: **£750**)

Tallying all of the above up: the total cost we are looking at here is **approximately £8,500** across the total five years. And that's with me underestimating some of the costs here to give a bit of leeway—most notably school uniform (which I can remember totalling up to more like £250 each year for my mum) and school trips. The latter largely depends on your financial position, as those with more money to spare will ultimately end up spending greater amounts on school trips—although for me myself, I know my friends (who continued going to my middle-class school through till the end of Year 11) went on some trips that were up in the thousands, with additional deposits in the high hundreds.

Now, our average of **£2,135.00** for a private candidate sitting five GCSEs probably looks borderline humorous. Even doubling this number to the average ten GCSEs a UK student will complete, our new figure of **£4,270** is literally 50% of what we'd spend on mainstream schooling—and that's *with* DLPs for every single subject, which every home-schooler likely wouldn't choose to do.

To put this into even *more* context: the average UK family will earn a total income of £30,000 a year—and so, with mainstream schooling, they'll be spending **5.5%** of their yearly income on **one** child, compared to **1.4%** for a home-schooled child.

These figures (shocking as they may be!) at least provide us with a very clear and solid conclusion: **home-schooling is considerably less financially demanding than mainstream schooling**. Such a finding really solidifies the sense of unity and indiscrimination we built surrounding home-schooling in our introduction: regardless of whether it actually would end up being the most beneficial option for a certain individual, there is no denying the fact that the *possibility* of home-schooling is open to every single person—

from every single age, degree of intelligence, and, in this case, socioeconomic position.

From all of the above we have explored, it seems very safe to say that our myth of home-schooling being more expensive than public schooling is very much so debunked.

ROUTINE: THE IMPORTANCE OF CONSISTENCY

W E MENTIONED IN OUR **Pros and Cons** section that one of the negatives of home-schooling oftentimes includes the 'transition' period that comes with transferring from mainstream schooling to independent learning—and it is my experience that the main reason why this is so frequently an issue surrounds the implementing of (or, rather, lack of implementing) the subject of this section: routine.

Now, the notion of routine—especially for us students!— is usually approached wearily... as an understatement. I know that during my days in school, I associated the things comprising my routine with the monotonous and unenjoyable yet necessary aspects of my day that I quite frankly dreaded: things like getting up at 7am, being in a specific classroom at a specific time, getting the bus after school... We all know the deal.

Indeed, even those of us who actually enjoy some form of structure in our lives usually find ourselves despising the repetitive dullness that comes with day-to-day responsibilities: after all, there comes a point when staring out your rain-spattered window to the same old grey scene every morning whilst in the midst of the congestion of 9am rush hour loses its appeal. Who wouldn't prefer to be in bed?

It is because of this that we all look forward to special occasions so much: whether that be your yearly holiday to Lanzarote, the Christmas period, or simply the relaxation of weekend. These are times that routine very much so takes a backseat, and we simply enjoy each moment as it comes— usually in the company of other people who are doing the same thing.

Whilst these latter times are certainly moments of occasion that are inherently very exciting and should be looked forward to (after all, it's always nice to count down to something), it should also not be these things that get you up in the morning: it is—as cheesy as it sounds—the possibilities of the day ahead of you that should be your primary motivator—the same motivator you associate with those times of special occasion.

But surely it's routine that obstructs these feelings from being a daily occurrence? After all, the common denominator with Lanzarote, Christmas, and the occupations of your Saturday evening, is that *you have no responsibilities or routine to adhere to*—right? Routine is surely a barrier to those things being a daily occurrence, not a facilitator. After all, you're always at your happiest when you're implementing no routine at all.

Wrong.

I invite you to cast your mind back to your most recent Christmas or summer break, or any other recent extended time period in which you associate your happiness with having no routine. You may think of a specific moment during that time period—maybe how great the food you ate was, or a specific activity your group all participated in—, but instead, I want you to think about what occurred during the *end* of those periods—when all the excitement had eventually died down, and the day's entertainment had ceased.

'Aimlessness' is the word that comes to mind for me to describe this time. A prime example of this for me is the six-week summer holiday, from July to September, that I would look forward to every single school year without fail, with promises of holidays to attend, books to read, and sunshine to soak. However, every year, without fail, would also invite that end-of-holiday, all-consuming boredom: suddenly, I'd be tired of feeling sluggish from my lie-ins, and—shocker!—I'd find myself actually missing my lessons and the mental stimulation it would provide—something that felt very welcome in the midst of the sticky, empty, end-of-summer days. This is a cycle I also watch my friends engage in every year: what starts as excitement for lack of responsibility ends with a craving for stability and direction.

Whilst this may not occur for every single one of such occasions for you, this is still a feeling *everybody* has experienced: whether that be the Sunday afternoon slump, or the lethargy that takes over when you've stayed out in the sun for a little too long on the eighth day of your holiday, we all begin to miss a sense of balance in our lives that follows a lengthy period of self-indulgence.

To put this into context even further, I am currently writing this whilst in the midst of the Coronavirus pandemic—and, with exams cancelled, schools closing down, and major restrictions with where we can go and when, my social media feed and inbox have been flooded with friends and acquaintances bored silly and feeling a complete lack of direction and purpose in day-to-day life. 3:30am is bedtime, 11:30am is when everyone rises, and the rest of the day passes with endless scrolling through social media, punctuated by the occasional dog walk.

Hopefully from this small exercise we can begin to see the importance that comes with some form of consistency and routine. However, that's not to say I am hoping to tell you to replicate a routine similar to that you'd have in school: rather, in this section, I hope to equip you with the tools required for you to construct a schedule that is as stable as it is flexible, offering enough variation and balance for you to remain both inspired and focused, grounded and ambitious, on a day-to-day basis.

Still not convinced you need to have such a schedule in place? Then let's consult the experts: individuals such as Benjamin Franklin and Leonardo Da Vinci, to Oprah Winfrey and Steve Jobs, swear by consistent, mindful, and productive daily routines (some being more stringent and niche than others—not to name names, Da Vinci). Plus, whilst we won't be listing them here, I strongly suggest you look into the (many hundreds) of studies online showcasing the reams of benefits that have been shown, time after time, to arise as a result of productive and sustainable (yet flexible) daily routines—it's pretty mind-blowing stuff.

An implicit running theme in our discussion of scheduling and routine, as you may notice as you progress through this section, is that of **mindset**. If there's one thing I have learnt over the course of my home-schooling journey, it's that **everything you do should centre around building upon your positive mindset**, and, in my experience, having a consistent, productive, and sustainable routine will encourage this more than anything else in your home-schooling journey. Hence, before we actually go into the specifics of what your routine should comprise in order to encourage this, I highly advise that you download The Self-Learners' Manifesto here:

https://www.fayepaige.co/readersfreebie.

This is simply a little reminder to yourself of what you're worth, the values you deserve to upkeep in your home-schooling journey, and the toxic, unproductive habits we have likely built over the past few years that we're going to be leaving behind us from this day forward. Stick it somewhere you'll be able to see often to remind yourself of these things as a promise to yourself and watch the magic unfold.

What I'm essentially getting at is that the routine you accumulate over your home-schooling journey—whether that be intentionally or unintentionally crafted—*will* completely shape your life, either for the better or the worst. It will influence your outlook on life and your studies, and the endless stretches of time at your disposal will either become your best friend or your worst enemy, depending on how you go about using the following information.

Consider all that is brought up in this section with an open mind, and I promise you that the possibilities of your home-schooling career will suddenly appear to take shape.

The Essential Ingredients

Now that we've established the *why* of developing a routine, let's delve into the *what*—that is, what are the things that should be at the foundation of your daily schedule?

The things I have listed below are, I would say, the **absolute non-negotiables of a successful daily routine**, especially when it comes to **adolescents and adults** that are looking at home-schooling. **Parents reading for their young children can skip this section entirely**: the suggested schedule explored in this section primarily focuses on encouraging mindfulness and discipline from the day's onset, and this would be better encouraged in children through a **loose yet consistent structure** (such as that outlined in the **Charlotte Mason Method**, discussed in our **Routes of Home-Schooling** section) that isn't quite as specific as what is explored below.

These are the things that I can always feel a very noticeable, drastic negative difference when I *don't* apply them—and when I *do*, the rest of my day is basically guaranteed to go as smoothly as it possibly could.

One thing before we delve into what these apparently magical things are: the vast majority of these things will probably seem pretty intuitive, and will also be things you'll have undoubtedly heard before. They are also things that will seem pretty easy to implement on the surface—which they *are*, technically speaking, but they also require **effort** on your part.

My reason for mentioning this is the fact that we can all get pretty lazy in terms of our mindset towards these things: we think they sound so simple that a) we tend to kid ourselves into thinking we *choose* not to do these things (when in the vast majority of cases, we don't at all—most of us struggle with self-discipline and need time to craft these habits); and b) that they **wouldn't make that much difference anyway**.

Whilst this mindset is understandable, it's ultimately false—and that is why I encourage you to remain as open-minded as possible. Grab a pen and paper and actively set out to implement the following habits, and you will be on track to becoming the best possible version of yourself—yes, really.

Sleeping Early, Rising Early

Did you see this one coming? Every health expert, CEO, life coach—you name it—seems to drill on about the importance of a consistent sleeping schedule—and this guide is no exception.

Going to bed and getting up early is the first piece of advice I always give to my friends when they are feeling demotivated, low, and adrift. This is, in my opinion, the most important thing on this list, and the best possible habit you can develop for your productivity, mental and physical health, and daily motivation. Consistently going to bed and getting up at a certain time regulates your body clock and boosts your metabolism, and those who rise early are consistently found to be more productive, proactive, and overall more positive than those who get up 'late'.

However, out of all I am about to give you, this seems to be the piece of advice people rebel over the most: I'm a night owl; I'm always in the worst mood in the morning; I'm most productive in the afternoon; I never feel like I've gotten enough sleep if I'm up before 10am... The list goes on and on.

Here's the long and short of it: **nobody can't train themselves to be a morning person**. The process of physically getting out of bed is admittedly rarely enjoyable, but once that's done, who wouldn't love to have the whole morning—one, perhaps two hours of pure quiet alone time, completely dedicated to whatever you want to do—stretched out in front of them? Literally nobody!

I speak from experience when I say that the morning is a truly beautiful time—that is, when you're not too exhausted to enjoy it! I began waking up at 4:30am every day (out of choice!) when I was 14, and I look back on the space between 5am and 7:30am with so much genuine happiness. It is serene, still, and frankly indescribable in terms of the genuine inner peace it can bring—and it allows you to be ten steps ahead of everyone else before they have even woken up. I can remember so many instances of watching the dawn, either outside or from my window, and being in awe of the fact that most actually *chose* not to experience this every day.

Now, I'm not suggesting you completely throw yourself into the deep end and commit to waking up at 4:30am every day; whilst that would be an incredible end goal, that would feel incredibly daunting to begin with. So what time *is* a good start? When should you be aiming to wake up in the morning? Go to any business magazine and they will seem to recommend every time under the sun, from 4am to 6am to 9am. So what is the 'correct' time?

This is going to vary slightly for each person, but it will absolutely be **before 7am**—that I can tell you as a fact. The time you wake up should also be around **1.5 hours** before you have any commitments—and by that I don't mean hard fast plans, but before you would normally need to start getting *ready* for those plans. This is so that you won't get the same feeling of dread waking up that you would normally have when getting up at 7am on a school morning: instead of having to run around and get everything sorted in the space of an hour (or less), you have 1.5 hours before you are obligated to do literally anything—and that is the magic of this strategy.

So, during that time when I was 14, I had a paper round that I had to leave for at around 7am—meaning I would normally need to start getting ready for the day (i.e., getting showered and dressed, having breakfast, etc.) at around 6am. Subtract 1.5 hours from this, and we get the time 4:30am.

What if you're lucky enough to have *no* commitments in the morning? We are talking about home-school, after all. In this case, you are able to find your **sweet spot**—that is, the time that you will feel most motivated and positive. *Everybody* has a sweet spot time for waking up—and, again, I can tell you this is always before 7am. This is when you feel ahead of the game and genuinely excited for the day ahead of you. It is also the time you will (whether you know about it yet or not) feel the most naturally energised. For some people, this could be as early as 4am; for others, it may be 6:45am.

So how do you find your sweet spot? You simply edge back your sleep schedule in small chunks—perhaps 15 minutes at a time—and see what time feels the best. This may sound a little vague, but once you get into the swing of getting up early, it starts being pretty intuitive: if I get up at 6:30am now, I still feel just as sluggish as if I'd risen at 9am. My sweet spot is between 4:30am and 5am, and generally speaking, **most sweet spots occur between 4:15am and 6am.**

What about going to bed? Going to bed at the right time is just as—if not more—important as getting up at the right time, as **your morning starts the night before**. Simply, you need to adjust the time you go to bed in line with when you wake up. You should be getting **a minimum of 7 hours of sleep**, although most of us perform most optimally with **between 7.5 and 9 hours of solid sleep**. You should also ditch your phone—or any other electronics—in the half hour before you go to bed: instead, read a book, write in a journal, meditate... These things sound redundant and like they wouldn't make too much difference, but in reality, these things will drastically impact your quality of sleep.

Find your sweet spot, be consistent with your bedtime and rising time, and you, my friend, are off to a truly amazing start.

Inner Peace and Personal Projects
So, you're up and awake before daybreak, and you have nothing but time stretching before you: now what?

There is a debate concerning what you should do first thing in the morning: some laud rolling out of bed and logging straight onto your computer to begin with work; others suggest exercise; some simply say to take the morning as it comes.

Here is what I've found, and will be saying till the end of time: your **first wakeful half hour should be entirely dedicated to your own inner peace**. Whilst this may sound strange and a bit vague (and maybe even entirely ridiculous to the cynic!), I encourage you to take a moment and think about when you feel truly at *peace*. This may, indeed, be during exercise; or perhaps it is whilst engaging in creative writing, or creating art.

For most, this answer will be almost instantaneous: it is usually the thing we love the most in the world, but somehow always ends up at the bottom of the list of our priorities. For me, this is meditation and reading. If you don't have an immediate answer, then I suggest dabbling in yoga, meditation, reading, writing, and early morning walks.

This is the thing that sets your soul on fire, and yet **doesn't take much physical or mental effort**. That is the key here: you need to ease yourself into the morning, doing something that brings you real happiness and will set you off on the right foot for the rest of the day, and yet won't feel daunting or overly tiring for when you're half asleep once that alarm has gone off.

After that first half hour, you will have an additional hour (at a minimum) at your disposal before the day's commitments begin. Now your brain is far more awake, my advice is to engage in **personal projects**. These are, again, things that you usually 'struggle for time for', and can include learning a new language, navigating new business pursuits, writing... These are things that are entirely for your own enjoyment, which may or may not be academic-/work-related in nature.

Alternatively, you could get a head-start on work at this point—although if you do decide to take this route, I suggest less mentally taxing tasks yet ones that will still provide you with a head-start, such as planning your day or responding to emails.

Doing these things first thing in the morning will give you a real sense of self-awareness, and, considering how simple they actually are, they are practically guaranteed to have a massive positive knock-on effect on the rest of your day.

Getting Dressed

This may seem like an odd one—and, if I were to choose anything on this list that will probably come across as being the most redundant to readers, it would be this one.

However, getting yourself physically ready for the day is absolutely essential when it comes to getting in the mindset for work—especially when we are talking in the context of home-schooling, where, in most cases, you will be staying entirely at home—a place usually associated with relaxation.

Indeed, one of my most commonly asked questions regarding home-schooling is **how to even get motivated to begin work in the first place**—and my answer to this is simple: get yourself dressed, as you would if you had to physically go to school or work. If you treat the day as if it *were* a workday, it automatically becomes one. Stay in your pyjamas and you're setting off a tidal wave of psychological responses signalling that it's time for relaxation, not time for work.

I would also say loungewear—a more socially acceptable step up from pyjamas—is also a no-no. Don't get me wrong, you don't need to go full business-casual when you're staying in your bedroom—but still, ditching the jogging bottoms for some jeans or pants would not go amiss. It's all about what you're feeding to your subconscious, and if you're lounging in the same clothes you've associated since the beginning of time with sleeping, then you're not exactly putting yourself in the best position to blaze through a to-do list (more on those in a moment)—especially if you're only just getting yourself accustomed to early mornings!

Moral of the story: ditch the onesie and fluffy socks. **If you wouldn't wear it to work or school, don't wear it now.** Sounds harsh and perhaps a bit unnecessary, but follow my advice and rare pyjama days will quickly get you feeling icky—trust me.

Phones

This is our last and—at least in the case of my age demographic and up—the most make-or-break aspect of your home-schooling routine—or, as a matter of fact, *any* task you want to commit to that requires any degree of focus. It is the dreaded no-nonsense phone conversation.

Whilst most of us would like to think we are not reliant on—or, to put it bluntly, addicted to—our devices, current statistics show that around **59% of adolescents are addicted to their phones**, according to their parents. In this same vein, the average daily screen time for this age group is currently a whopping **7 hours and 22 minutes**, that for 8- to 12-year-olds being **4 hours and 44 minutes**.

What does this have to do with home-schooling? The relevance lies in not how *much* we're on our phones, but *when*. If going on your phone is your form of downtime, that is neither here nor there when it comes to how productive your time spent home-schooling is—so long as it *is* during that specified downtime that you're using your phone. Indeed, whilst most of us (me included!) would probably assume most of our phone use would be during the weekend and in the evenings after work, it's actually surfaced that the vast majority of us spend just as much time on our phones in the middle of the day **during work** as we do during weekends.

This has a massive spiral effect in terms of our productivity during worktime, as out of the **58 times** the average adult picks up their phone daily, **30 of those are during work hours**—and, whilst this might not sound like a lot to some, this leads to an average of **1.6 hours of total screen time during work**, just from pickups.

Not only is this a hefty chunk of time taken from your workday, but this is also a major disruption to your **sense of flow** during work—something we'll be covering in more depth in a moment, as it is absolutely paramount for extended periods of productive work.

Because of this, it is essential we are super stringent with our phone use during school/worktime. Whilst there are a load of apps on the market restricting phone use, I have personally found it to be more effective to just cut to the chase: turn that baby off completely. Putting it on Flight Mode/Do Not Disturb is, in my experience, about as effective as simply leaving it across the room (read: not at all), as is disabling notifications. By all means try these out if they sound promising to you, but I'm not guaranteeing you a major reduction in your daytime screen time with these methods; I *am*, however, guaranteeing you results if you turn it off and chuck it somewhere awkward—maybe under a mattress, or in a bread bin downstairs. Whatever works; just get that thing far away from you. Don't simply reduce the temptation: eliminate it completely.

This is something I have been doing for a few years now, and is something I wish I had just implemented from the get-go—not just with home-schooling, but with family events, my non-phone-related downtime... Literally anything requiring my attention in any form. It's not as scary as it sounds, trust me, and you'll be reaping the benefits in no time—and preaching them to everyone you know soon after, no doubt!

Essentially, **consciously committing your mind fully to the task at hand** is a habit that will take some time to build—and by 'some time', I mean around a week or two *without* regular phone use, and potentially *never* with. Yes, it really is that important!

Before we continue, I would like to stress (yet again) the importance behind all of the tips listed above (and in the downloadable I'm going to direct you to below): all are grounded not just from my own experience, but from reams and reams of psychological research concerning not just productivity and success, but also the encouraging of traits such as tenacity, rigour, positivity, and self-confidence. It was from the point of my conscious implementation of all of the above on a daily basis from the age of 14 that I started to experience a serious tangible shift in terms of my approach to life—a shift that is very much so within reach for everybody, with the implementation of the above.

Of course, we have not yet delved into the specificities of what your timetable during the *workday* should actually include; we'll be going into that below. The importance of a truly productive, sustainable, and, above all, *enjoyable* schedule, however, lies in not what the end result is—i.e., what is actually *within* the timetable—, but the manner in which its construction is approached—and it is an intuition for this that I hope we have developed by studying the above.

All this may sound overly philosophical for a simple schedule, but it is such mindfulness and self-awareness that will be what propels you forward in the long-term to achieve big things—and this is where the true magic and potential of home-schooling lies. With such an approach, you are not just going to **survive** home-schooling in the same way you would have mainstream schooling, but **thrive** and bring your pursuits and aspirations to all-new heights.

The full development of this mindset is the first and most crucial step of achieving your full potential in home-education (hence the chronology of this chapter), and is something I go into far more depth over in the first module of The Learning Success Academy, my online self-teaching program—all with the aim of guaranteeing your achievement of true excellence from the onset of your home-schooling journey.

Now, we're going to be going into some *real* depth in this section concerning your actual school routine (as we should; it forms the foundation of your entire learning experience, after all!), so before we dive right in, ensure you've downloaded and had a quick read through my Top 3 Mistakes Home-Schoolers Make When Scheduling downloadable (available here: https://www.fayepaige.co/readersfreebie) if you haven't already, as this will set the tone nicely for what we're going to be covering here. It's only a ten-minute read (if that), don't worry, and will help everything we're going to explore next connect to form a bigger picture and purpose... Plus, you may even get some exclusive content in your inbox that will guarantee that you become even *more* of a boss in your newfound schedule ;)

If you currently feel excited—or even slightly less sceptical than the beginning of this chapter!—regarding the formulation of such an approach to life and your studies, then I am very satisfied indeed, and we are off to a fantastic start.

With that being said, let us go into the specifics of how to actually create a daily schedule.

Actually Constructing a Schedule

So, we have formed—or are looking at forming—the daily habits integral to ensuring the smooth use of a productive and gratifying schedule—but what should that schedule actually include? How should we go about even creating one?

These were questions that plagued me during my first couple of years of home-schooling before I truly got to grips with what worked for me—and are, indeed, the questions that have preoccupied every other home-schooler I have ever spoken to during their initial transition to home-education. The vast majority of us can most likely agree (whether it hindered our academic progress significantly or not) that the structure implemented by the majority of mainstream schools is not optimal: rather than moulding the routine around its students and what is most productive for them, students are forced to mould themselves around a predetermined schedule, constructed for the sole purpose of ticking all the boxes of a given—again, predetermined—curriculum provided by the government.

This is, clearly, *not* something we are looking at replicating now that we have full control of the hours in our days. In other words, we know what *not* to do—or, rather, the general feelings we do not want to replicate—within our new way of life. Even if you are looking at ticking the same boxes as a mainstream school (e.g., if you're following the exact same GCSE curricula), you don't want these same feelings of monotony and dread surrounding your own academic pursuits.

So if your schedule were to be comprised of essentially the **same tasks** (this is just a for-instance—you may very well not be following the national curriculum), how on earth could we create the **opposite feelings and attitudes**? Is this even possible?

The answer is yes, and, as much as there is far more we could delve into here, in order to keep this section condensed and concise, we will instead be tackling two key themes that will allow you to get potentially identical things done, but in a way that is completely tailored to you: **balance** and **structure**.

Attaining Balance

This aspect of constructing a schedule is (as is the case with, admittedly, all that has been and will be discussed thus far) a major make-or-break aspect of any schedule, this time in terms of **sustainability**.

'Balance' in this context basically refers to **how you distribute your time**, and across which tasks—not only in terms of getting equal amounts of **work and play time**, but also balance in terms of **the nature of the work itself**. Those who attain balance within their work tend to stay motivated for very extended periods of time and are at a very low risk of **burnout** (the **learning slump**). On the contrary, those who *don't* achieve a sense of balance in their work frequently lack sufficient motivation, procrastinate more, and, when they *do* get down to it, don't enjoy their work nearly as much as they otherwise would. This can also take a toll on other aspects of your life, including your interpersonal relationships, overall mood, and your self-esteem.

This has been tried and tested by none other than yours truly. As I'm sure all my close friends and family can attest, striking a good balance between work and play has been the aspect of home-schooling I have struggled with the most. As I'm sure my fellow high achievers can understand, I have always been a culprit of confusing **overwork** with **productivity**—when in reality, working too much is often just as unproductive as working too little, in the sense that it massively compensates on the quality of work produced. When I was 12 years old and studying for a Level 4 diploma in psychology (which is, in terms of difficulty, somewhere between A-Levels and the first year of a degree, and was a sort of 'step up' from the Level 3 one I referred to earlier), I worked **long but unproductive hours**: with no experience whatsoever on how to revise, I would spend between six and 12 hours three days a week handwriting out around 8,000 words of my lesson content before converting this information to flashcards and cram learning it the night before my end-of-module tests. Whilst this certainly got me high grades and paid off academically in the short-term, it meant I had little to no down time on a daily basis, which eventually took a toll on my mental health and my perception of my own self-worth.

Indeed, situations equivalent to this—whether it's on the same end of the scale or not—are super easy to get into when you're in the driver's seat of your routine. For someone like me who had been obsessive over working long hours while *in* the restraints of a school timetable, this sudden complete control was bound to lead to disaster without some guidance—and that's what an awareness of balance is going to help you to avoid completely.

So, how do you attain balance in your daily life?

Our central concept here (which you may or may not already be familiar with) is the **8-8-8 rule**. This principle essentially tells us to organise our 24-hour day into three eight-hour sections: one being spent sleeping, one being spent on work, and one being spent on leisure.

This principle was pretty eye-opening to me the first time I learned of it, particularly when I cast my mind back to how I would typically spend my time and the 'categories' the way I spent my time would fall into. Suddenly, my four hours of daily average screen time seemed almost ludicrous—that was *half* of my leisure time right there—, as did, conversely, my previous 12-hour slogs of workdays.

This is a notion I highly advise you to keep in the back of your mind when scheduling your days (the structure of which we'll delve into in the next subsection): think about how you spend your precious eight hours of leisure time, and consider whether they are things you **genuinely enjoy** and **help you to recoup**. Begin holding yourself accountable for how you spend your spare time: how much do you spend doing the things you'd truly love to be doing? And how much is spent on the mundane and meaningless—the things you can openly admit mean absolutely nothing to you?

This is why having **personal projects** and out-of-work pursuits is so important, and something that was given much attention in our previous section. I, myself, have noticed a dramatic shift when I am actively pursuing personal projects versus when I'm not—whether that be small-scale projects/interests, like meditating frequently or learning the guitar, or bigger projects, like writing this book or kickstarting my own self-teaching business. It is essential we maintain a **sense of identity independent from our work life**, and it is this, primarily, that is going to help you not only **establish** but **maintain** a true sense of balance in your daily life.

In a similar vein, it's interesting then to analyse how we spend our eight-hour work slot: how much of it do we currently spend completely focused, committed, and efficient? And, on the contrary, how much of it is spent procrastinating, skimming over potentially demanding content, and getting distracted? What percentage of the work we complete do we fully absorb and benefit from later down the line? How much of what we do is **deep work**—work that is totally focused upon and deeply, meaningfully processed—, and how much makes little to no difference in terms of our understanding of a subject?

Knowing how you work is an absolutely essential and game-changing first step to being able to work deeply and productively—and, thus, I go into a) how to establish what kind of worker you are, and b) how to then realistically mould your working methods around this to promote the most productive work possible, in The Learning Success Academy—crafted specifically for you. However, as a starting point, I would like you to consider the following questions and make some notes of your answers:

- Do you tend to feel most focused during **extended** periods of **deep work**, or do you rely on frequent breaks to keep you motivated?
- What are some of your key distractors during work? How can you look at eliminating those distractors?
- Do you require variety in your workday to keep you stimulated (e.g., use of different mediums; changes in location; jumping between several subjects)? Are you currently applying these requirements to your schedule?
- Do your breaks currently lead to you feeling more energised and motivated to work, or do they lead to further procrastination?
- Is your current workspace conducive to productive work (e.g., quiet; clean; comfortable)?

Ensure you think deeply about the questions above and are completely honest with your answers, and we're well on our way to constructing a schedule based entirely on **your** work ethic, requirements, and way of thinking and processing information.

Now we have a more solid grasp on the elements you specifically need to incorporate into your daily life in order to strike a positive balance between work and play, let's delve into what kind of **structure** we should be looking at implementing.

Establishing Structure

We have established that in order to attain a sense of balance between work and play in your daily life, you should allocate your time evenly and mindfully across your work and the things that allow you to recoup and maintain a sense of identity. However, we have *also* established that you can work for extended periods of times unproductively, under the illusion that because you're *technically* working, that must mean you are being productive—when we of course know this not to be the case. With some of the answers you just jotted down, we should have a rough idea of the things we need to bear in mind when structuring our days—but here, we need to get more specific in order to garner a clear image of what a productive day would actually look like: not just how long is spent working, but what is actually done during that time.

It is here that an effective structure in terms of how you schedule your *work* is necessary, the overall goal here being to work productively, for extended periods of time, without feeling mentally exhausted by the end of it; indeed, if anything, we're aiming to feel inspired and energised after a workday, not drained.

We are going to achieve this through two avenues: **to-do lists** and **prioritising flow**.

Firstly, to-do lists. For how simple they are, to-do lists are truly magical things: they create a loose structure to your day and allow for your schedule to be as streamlined and straightforward as possible, whilst still providing far more flexibility than, say, an hour-by-hour timetable (such as the one you'd adhere to in school). Indeed, as touched on above, I struggled with maintaining both balance and structure in the first couple of years of my home-schooling—and, predictably, it was timetables I was using at this time. Whilst timetables can be effective, they pose the risk of being more discouraging than encouraging: get an unexpected urgent email through or spend an extra fifteen minutes on a task than expected and suddenly you're 'behind' and potentially stressed—even when you could easily get back on top of it!

It was when I transitioned to to-do lists (and started using them correctly!) that I found my studies to be far more successful—in terms of both productivity and sustainability. Hence, in order to ensure your use of to-do lists forms a solid basis for the day's productivity and doesn't have the opposite effect, here are the three essential elements of any to-do list:

- **Break your larger tasks down into smaller tasks**: For example, rather than writing 'Write Jane Austen Essay', split it further into 'Essay Introduction; Essay Paragraph 1; Essay Paragraph 2', etc. **Success leads to motivation leads to success**: in order for your work sessions to be productive and for you to get vast quantities completed efficiently, you're going to need **small successes** to keep your motivation levels high throughout and to avoid any larger tasks feeling like a slog.

- **Use approximate timescales**: The key word here is 'approximate': remember, we're not looking to replicate a stringent timetable. Pop a little approximation of the time you reckon it'll take for you to complete a task, and, as per the **8-8-8 Rule**, ensure your tasks in total do not overstep the maximum eight-hour mark. Prioritise **practicality over ambition**.

- **Do not begin your work session with a daunting task**: There is a wealth of debate surrounding what kind of task you should kickstart your day with; something difficult to provide you with a rush of motivation, or an easy one to ease you into the day? My advice would be a sort of in-between of these two arguments: your task should be something this is not hugely mentally taxing and daunting (or this will undoubtedly lend the way to procrastination), but will still make you feel highly motivated after completing it. One final element of structure meriting consideration before we move on: prioritising flow.

'Flow', officially dubbed by Dr Csikszentmihalyi, is defined as, 'The state of concentration and engagement that can be achieved when completing a task that challenges one's skills'. Most of us will have experienced flow before: it is that feeling of the world falling away as we grow so wrapped up in a task that the time seems to fly by, and occurs when we are completely focused on the task at hand, whatever that may be.

Flow is the magic touch for any given task, especially when it comes to independent learning. When in a state of flow, you can find a sense of rhythm in your work; it creates a feeling of complete relaxation and, in a way, comfort, lending the way to an almost meditative state.

It is this that I want you to prioritise, and it is this that was the basis of my questions in our previous subsection: create a comfortable workspace, pinpoint when your peaks and troughs in motivation tend to occur, and use breaks wisely, and a state of complete flow is very achievable.

Contrary to popular belief, you do not have to be somebody who can work three, five, seven hours at a time without needing a break in order to achieve flow. Flow is not about constant work; it is about *consistent* work, or the idea that when you *do* work, you do so in an utterly focused and dedicated way. Flow also extends to when you're *not* working: it's about maintaining that meditative state during breaks, meaning you stay 'in the zone' and completely motivated. As you'll probably be able to predict here, this means that I highly advise you to use your breaks with this as the priority; reading, walks, and conversations with others can promote this, although this will differ with everyone.

However, whilst you do not *need* to work for extended periods at a time in order to maintain flow, you'll most likely find that this state will increase your focus significantly and, thus, reduce your need for breaks or time off in order to recoup. It sounds like a paradox, but **the more you focus, the less time you'll tend to need off**—and this is, my friend, is the secret of every highly efficient and productive individual. Without flow, every work session would feel like an uphill battle and would be thoroughly unenjoyable, regardless of if the content was actually of interest to you.

It is a lack of flow and, hence, balance and structure, that leads to so many people burning out in jobs they'd otherwise love, and learning about subjects they'd otherwise find invigorating. It is a lack of flow that leads to any task feeling like a slog. It is also, on the contrary, a *presence* of flow that typically makes us so productive and stimulated when we first start out on a pursuit that appears promising—such as starting a new job, or learning a new subject or skill. Flow makes us feel confident and ahead of the game; a lack of it makes us feel useless and stuck in a rut.

The purpose of this section was to a) give you a very solid sense of direction in terms of formulating your daily schedule, and b) show you that, regardless of your current levels of productivity and/or motivation, it *is* possible for you to maintain focus and achieve every single goal that you set out (academic or not) by gradually building upon smaller daily habits tailored specifically to you.

To sum up all we have discussed in this section and apply it practically, I would like to remind you that *you*, my dear reader, have exclusive access to **my typical daily schedule**, free for download here:

https://www.fayepaige.co/readersfreebie.

This is to give you an idea of what a day using all of the above principles could actually look like. You may also wish to try out my personal schedule for a day and see how you go—what works for you, and what you'd change to suit you better. **This is not my stringent schedule**; I do not have a minute-by-minute or hour-by-hour plan for each day, as this would completely remove the flexibility and balance we're trying to attain within home-schooling. However, bearing in mind when I wake up, when I go to sleep, and when my levels of flow and motivation tend to be highest, this is how my days typically pan out implementing all of the discussed principles.

By implementing the above tips, we are not only ensuring that we work productively and tick an impressive list of tasks off our to-do lists each day, but also that we are actively caring for ourselves spiritually and mentally. Lucky for us, academic success and mental wellness often go hand-in-hand—only it's the mental wellness that has to come first. That's not to say those who are highly stressed or unhappy never achieve great things, but it's the not-so-subtle difference between working *with* and working *against* yourself that will **guarantee** you to work to the best of your ability always—not to mention the fact that it will do wonders for your confidence.

Worry not if you find it difficult to fully implement all of the above straight away: whilst the habits discussed are simple, they ultimately will, for the vast majority of us, require us to break habits we've had for a number of years—whether that be waking up late, spending too much time on play and too little on work (and vice versa), or overall transforming your mindset regarding how you approach each day. Be kind to yourself—and, in the wise words of Robert Louis Stevenson, 'Don't judge each day by the harvest you reap, but by the seeds that you plant.' Your active deciding to take the advice discussed here on-board is your first seed; and every step you take to action such advice from hereon out—whether that be commencing a new project separate from work, setting an alarm for half an hour earlier than you'd normally rise, or ditching the joggers when it hits 8am—is also a step in the right direction. Any progress is progress, and, if you ever feel that not to be the case, just remember it takes roughly **two months** to fully form a habit to the point where it becomes second nature. There is a very viable ending in sight!

AN END NOTE

THIS IS A BOOK I never planned to write.

Home-schooling had been great, but it wasn't something I was *passionate* about: sure, I valued my routine and my freedom and the direction my academics had taken, but that was just me—what I did on a daily basis. I was grateful for the independence I had been given, but—wrongfully—assumed anyone else in the same position would have found their way with home-schooling and wound up doing the same things I did, having found how effective they were.

It was, somewhat ironically, upon my *re-joining* school—specifically college at the age of 16, after a few months shy of five years being home-schooled—that my passion for effective education—and, in turn, this book—was born. I had loved home-schooling, but wanted to re-join mainstream education if anything out of curiosity: I had never been to school during my adolescence, and I hoped for a little more exposure to the social side of things—and was also interested to see for myself what I made of the education system, rather than hearing about it through my secondary source of my (biased) friends.

My experience was both eye-opening and underwhelming: for a reason I couldn't place at the time, my days felt so exhausting yet so under-stimulating and so *incomplete*. My school days spanned from 9am to 3:45pm— just under seven hours of socialising and learning—, and yet not once did I feel truly stimulated during the day. By the end of each day, whilst my body would be drained, my mind would have reached a dull buzz. The only time during my time in college that I would feel myself reach *any* state even close to flow, or true enjoyment, was during my extensive library study sessions—and even then, I found my focus wavered so much more than it ever had before; it was like by not pushing myself in mind of my own limits, my attention span had shortened considerably and my motivation had run dry.

I find this interesting, because I was by no means unhappy. My teachers were also by no means incompetent, and the content of my courses was extensive and detailed. I was a straight A (oftentimes A*) student during my time there and achieved a grade 9 (an A**) in GCSE English Language after six weeks of preparation, and so I didn't struggle academically, either.

So what was the problem? Sure, the institution I was in had changed—as had the structure of my days—, but I was still the same *person*, taking similar subjects to what I had done and enjoyed before. So what had triggered a change this dramatic?

I didn't reach a solid answer to this question up until very recently—some five months after leaving college and reverting back to home-schooling—, which is surprising considering its simplicity: I was **educated**, but I was not **cultured** or **nurtured** in any capacity. My adoration for learning, which had always stemmed from the spiderweb of knowledge at my disposal, everything relevant and interlinking and applicable to something so much bigger and more significant than me, was now reduced to a sort of tunnel vision that only prioritised getting a certain letter at the top of my next test. Having a firm intuition, passion, and depth of understanding for a subject was no longer what I was taught to prioritise: instead, I had to learn to replicate a textbook's robotic, staggered writing style and content in order to ensure my writing was 'concise' and less discussion-based. I would have to repress my urges to relate an extract's character's behaviour as something similar displayed in a psychological study because it 'wasn't on the specification'. Cross-referencing and making links between different disciplines wasn't allowed. Thinking abstractly at all was risky, and anything concrete I wrote had to relate directly to what an exam board deemed relevant.

You can get as many A*'s in a row as you like, but as soon as you're waiting at that bus stop with a sense of dread that you can't logically justify, you're fighting a losing battle. As soon as you find yourself repressing your creative urges—or, worse, losing them altogether—, you're allowing yourself to be put in a box.

I craved depth—academically and socially—, and yet found myself too bogged down by the day's trivialities to even try to find it.

Here, we can see that the problem didn't lie in solely my teachers, my friends, the content I was learning, the atmosphere I was in... Simply, it was the fact that I had previously (during home-schooling) crafted approaches and habits for learning that met my needs precisely—and, because no school or institution of any sort can accommodate for the specific needs for hundreds of diverse, independent people, there leaves only one option: force them to adapt, and leave behind what their minds really require.

It took me one (admittedly long-winded!) conversation with my mum one dreary Saturday afternoon in November for my intended path to become clear once again, before which point I hadn't even fleetingly seriously considered leaving school again: I needed to reclaim myself, and, unlike last time I'd left school, I actually knew the specific steps I would have to take this time in order to bring that to fruition.

Whether you're somebody currently deliberating leaving the education system, somebody that has already taken the plunge and yet has struggled with reaching a place of fulfilment, or a parent looking to engage their child in their studies more, I sincerely hope this book has provided you with the latter feeling—the feeling 16-year-old Faye experienced when she walked out school doors for the last time, the world at her feet—than one more reminiscent of 11-year-old Faye—hopeful and enthusiastic, but adrift and overwhelmed with the power and responsibility suddenly placed on her shoulders.

If this is the case for you, I would highly encourage you to check out any of the downloadables I have referenced throughout this book, as these are not only super valuable in and of themselves, but they will also provide you with a little taster of the kind of approach I take with my students in The Learning Success Academy, my online self-teaching program teaching home-schoolers basically everything covered in this book, only in *way* more depth and with a ton of extra material. My entire goal is to equip my students with enough knowledge and strategies that they are left in a position to formulate for themselves, in mind of their own strengths, weaknesses, goals, priorities, and circumstances, an approach that essentially guarantees their fulfilling of their own potential—whatever that may look like for them. Each individual's learning experience will always be completely unique, regardless of whether you try to put them in a box or not, and so my personal aim is to embrace such differences in my learners and allow them to create a tailored approach for themselves.

Learning, knowledge, and education have no boundaries—although through standardisation and a demand for conformity, the education system would, for the most part, have us thinking the opposite. This has lent the way to a pandemic of graduates who, despite thousands of hours of study, struggle to navigate the fundamental problems of human nature—objects of discussion since before Christ.

Let us favour intuition over memorisation; individualism over traditionalism; passion over curriculum. Let us create a culture where academia is associated with a sense of power and exhilaration, rather than dread and stress. Let us embrace the arts alongside the sciences, and appreciate how the deeper we delve into both, the more they entangle in one another, and regard them both in equal measure. Let us use standardised testing not as an end point, but as an indication of understanding—and only where suitable.

Here's to a change in mindset and approach. And here's to a learning process not just engaged in the *task* of learning, but also in the *result* of it—however small those little successes may be.

MY FREE RESOURCES

OVER THE COURSE OF this book, I have mentioned a wealth of resources that I created myself in light of my own experiences (and struggles!) with home-schooling so you can set off on the right track; so, in order to enable you to access these super easily in the future, I have compiled all such references in the list below. I hope you find these as helpful as I have, and that they help you feel better equipped in re/starting your home-schooling journey going forward!

The Top 3 Rookie Mistakes Home-Schoolers Make When Scheduling:

https://www.fayepaige.co/readersfreebie

The Self-Learner's Manifesto

https://www.fayepaige.co/readersfreebie

The Faye Paige Schedule

https://www.fayepaige.co/readersfreebie